The Art of Non-Expert Living

By

Oberon Michaels

Copyright © Oberon Michaels

All rights reserved. No part of this book may be reproduced in any form without written permission from the rights holder, apart from short excepts to be used in reviews or for the purpose of publicity.

Cover design by Oberon Michaels.

Contents

Introduction 7
    Why this book has been written 8
    The Basic Principles 13
    Expertise 22

Chapter 1: Buddhist Theory 28
    Essential Buddhist Principles 29
    The Three Signs of Being 31
    The Three Fires 46
    The Five Skandhas 51
    The Four Noble Truths 56

Chapter 2: The Buddhist Background 60
    Buddhism: An Outline 61
    Zen: a historical view 66
    Zen in practice 76
    The Heart Sutra 88

Chapter 3: The Path 94
    How hard should life be? 95
    Truth 98
    Freedom 103

Faith	106
Revelation	112
Salvation	118
Sin	128
Worship	147
Liberation	151
Chapter 4: Strategies	164
A menu of options	165
What drives us?	165
The Three Modes of Choice	170
Attitude	174
Hacking the Universe	185
Goal Setting	189
Pathology	193
Putting it all together	199
Chapter 5: Meditation	204
Meditation and visualization	205
Conclusion	216
Goodbye for now	217
Bibliography	220

Introduction

Why this book has been written

Civilization has greatly benefited from specialization – in fact, it may be said that all advances in education, science, technology, transport, communication, and standards of living would have been impossible without the development of specialized skills.

Most people are quite happy to call on the services of experts in various areas of life. When a fire breaks out, we call the fire service; we take our vehicles to a mechanic for repairs and servicing, and sometimes to a specialist mechanic if the vehicle is particularly exotic; if we experience a severe toothache, we usually consult a dentist; if we are threatened with legal action, we seek the services of a lawyer. Should we discover that one of these practitioners lacks the appropriate qualifications or is a fraud, we become indignant, feeling that our trust has been betrayed believing that regulatory action should be taken to exclude such operators from the profession.

However, there is one aspect of life in which the issue of the support of experts becomes problematic. This area could be loosely defined as personal life management ie. optimizing one's choices and lifestyle for optimum success and happiness. A vast array of practitioners claim to offer specialized services in this arena, including:

- Teachers
- Psychiatrists
- Psychologists
- Counselors
- Pastors

- Priests
- Shamans
- Life coaches

The issue of appropriate qualifications for such services is peculiarly complex because generally, the most that can be offered is advice. Interpreting and acting on such advice is up to the person receiving the advice. A further complication is that the perception of problems and the judging of the success of the strategies applied are essentially subjective. If a person is suffering from a broken leg, the success of any treatment is easy to establish. On the other hand, the assessment of the causes of many psychological complaints and the effectiveness of any treatment can be a difficult and complex matter.

It is nonsensical to expect another person to interpret how you feel. Furthermore, it is dangerous to rely entirely on others to determine the cause of any psychological inharmony or deficiency in your life. Everyone has a personal worldview that has been developed from various influences which can include natural aptitude, the family of origin, social standing, education, religious beliefs, physical health, and life experience.

Expertise results from instruction and experience. But a new discipline or body of knowledge is created from the position of non-expertise. For example, when Isaac Newton developed the calculus, he did not have previous expertise in it. Similarly, with many dimensions of common life, like parenting, no-one starts from a position of expertise. The most effective learning always starts from an assumption that one is not at all conversant in a particular area. As life is an unpredictable process and offers unique opportunities to each person, the process of navigating this psychological obstacle course will also be unique. Whether we like it or not, life is a process of continuous learning and self-instruction requires a person to go where he or she has never been before.

Everyone is entitled to pursue a lifestyle that is healthy, joyful, productive, socially responsible and that appropriately accommodates the views, needs, and plans of others. *The Art of Non-expert Living* is about managing those aspects of your life in which you are the expert. You are the only person who truly knows:

- How you feel
- What gives you joy
- What you dislike
- What you fear
- What gives you a sense of fulfilment
- Your memory of the past
- Your expectations of the future

One of the most problematic influences in the conduct of daily life is probably that of religious beliefs, which are, in many cases, socially determined. I see organized religion as a cultural artefact, as are language, music, literature, and social customs. In many cases, it expresses what we want to believe and what we want others to believe, rather than what really is. As Einstein said, we should seek to see the world as it is, not as we would prefer it to be.

Non-expert living is opposed to the canonization of scriptural texts as a basis for regulating one's life. Such canonization severely limits the life-options of a person by insisting that a particular cultural artefact is perfect and without error and that it comprehensively and adequately addresses all the important issues of life. The obvious example can be found in the Bible. If a person detects an error in such a source, or finds it confusing, an assumption may be made that the person rather than the artefact is at fault; hence he or she should either commit to further study or just accept the received wisdom as having been delivered by a much wiser being. In a 2015 talk called "Exploring the Tension Between Calvinists and Arminians," Calvinist preacher John Piper described his attitude toward difficulties in scripture in this way: "There must be something wrong with my head. I see what's in the text, and I say my head's the problem. I'm the problem – not the Bible." But often, theology is a form of philosophical speculation where the conclusions derived are unfalsifiable opinions that can be a source of great disagreement.

This book is not a primer on how to attain enlightenment. Although much of the material has been drawn from Buddhist theory, it is not a manual on Buddhist practice. Non-expert living is that beast so much despised by the religious apologist: a syncretic system, comprised of elements drawn from various religious philosophies as well as several self-help modalities and theories. I am open to the criticism of having cherry-picked the ideas and strategies which suit me personally. I am happy to confess that this has been my approach – but in my view, it has also been the approach of all religious systems as well. They, like literature, philosophy, and music, are also the results of the synthesis of aspects of cultural and social evolution.

The views expressed and the strategies described in this book are my own and describe what I believe has worked best for me. Not all of these may suit other people, and some may reject them as untenable or even false. Nor should the opinions and conclusions I have derived from research into religion, psychology, history, or self-help therapies be considered authoritative statements. For an informed opinion on any of these subjects a recognized expert should be consulted.

The tools and strategies I have suggested are for people who are in reasonably good health and generally have a good handle on running their own lives. Their primary purpose is to provide an enhanced sense of well-being. They are not a substitute for professional medical treatment or therapy. Anyone receiving such treatment should continue to follow the advice of their treating health practitioner.

The Basic Principles

The principles of Non-expert Living have been drawn from many sources. Hence it is a syncretic system of the sort that is despised by advocates of deterministic theology and philosophy which claim to be consistent, integral, and pure in their structure. These assertions are not supportable when one considers the current of history and the evolution of worldviews. In the pre-Christian era, Judaism was a tribal faith that focused on developing a relationship with an accessible deity to obtain political or personal advantage. Relatively little attention was placed on the afterlife and the eventual fate of individuals. During the exile in the Persian diaspora in the Sixth Century BCE, Jewish theologians were influenced by Zoroastrianism, in which the afterlife and the conflict between good and evil supervising deities loomed large. As a result, the view of this life as a path to the next became more pervasive.

Christianity developed as a sect of Judaism and claimed to derive its essential validity as the consummation of Jewish religious history. It retained the concept of a covenant between God and a select group of people, but claimed that those who rejected the refurbished covenant would be excluded from salvation. Islam borrowed many stories, doctrines, and personages from Christianity, and has been viewed by some as a Christian heresy. For example, Doctor of the Catholic Church, John of Damascus (675 – 749) in his book "On Heresies" states, "

From that time to the present a false prophet named Mohammed has appeared in their midst. This man, after having chanced upon the Old and New Testaments and likewise, it seems, having conversed with an Arian monk, devised his own heresy. Then, having insinuated himself into the good graces of the people by a show of seeming piety, he gave out that a certain book had been sent down to him from heaven. He had set down some ridiculous compositions in this book of his and he gave it to them as an object of veneration.

Thomas Aquinas (1225 – 1274) sought to recognize the principles identified by Aristotle with Christian theology, and, ironically, stimulated a tradition of intellectual inquiry that eventually resulted in the Enlightenment.

Further to the East, Buddhism absorbed many principles from Hinduism, notably liberation and reincarnation.

Hence, syncretism can be seen as a natural an inevitable process in the development of religious thought. Non-Expert Living honors this approach by incorporating concepts from Buddhism and various philosophies which have been contemptuously dismissed as "New Age." The figures that have most influenced me are those who eschewed automatic subscription to a set system of beliefs and sought to work out a worldview from scratch. The most eminent of these is Buddha. By contrast, other figures like the Hebrew patriarchs and prophets, Christ, Mohammed, and the church fathers used existing practices and philosophies as launching pads for the propagation of deterministic systems of belief, and consequently, their teachings lack genuine universality and applicability.

The principles identified below illustrate the structure of Non-Expert Living. People wishing to apply any of the strategies described are not required to subscribe to any particular belief and are free to disagree with any of the theories put forward.

Principles derived from Buddhism

The following foundation principles of Non-Expert Living have been drawn from classical Buddhist philosophy. Each of these is discussed at length in Part 2 of this book – Essential Buddhist Theory.

One of the most appealing features of Buddhism, as opposed to many other religions, is that it accepts the fact that in an ideal world it would become redundant. When all sentient beings become enlightened, there will be no further need for religion. By contrast, religions that are modalities for gaining the best place in the next world usually propose a very denominational afterlife – the Christians have a Christian Heaven and the Muslims an Islamic Paradise. There is the old joke about the Methodist who went to heaven. As he looked around, he noticed a massive wall enclosing a large tract of ground. Upon inquiry, he was told: "That is the precinct for Roman Catholics; they like to believe that they are the only ones up here."

The Three Signs of Being

- Impermanence
- Misery (Discontent)
- Absence of self-nature

The Three Fires

- Attraction
- Aversion
- Ignorance

The Four Noble Truths

These represent some of the most foundational and best-known principles of Buddhism. The focus is on understanding the state of the individual, rather than devoting oneself to, and being instructed by, a cosmic divinity and its representatives.

- Man is trapped in a ceaseless round of suffering;
- The cause of this suffering is unsatisfied desire;
- The path to true happiness is through the cessation of desire:
- This ultimate happiness can be achieved through the Noble Eightfold path.

The Noble Eightfold path involves:

- Right Understanding
- Right Intention
- Right Speech
- Right Conduct
- Right Livelihood
- Right Discipline
- Right Mindfulness
- Right Meditation

In this context, "right" means fitting or appropriate, rather than satisfying an externally devised, doctrinaire moral standard.

Although the process is described as a path, it does not mean that each element should be acquired or studied in progression. Rather, in each of these areas, the practitioner should seek to achieve the best realization of each of these qualities from the start.

The Five Skandhas or Aggregates.

These are the constituent parts of a functional human being.

- Form
- Sensation
- Perception
- Tendency
- Consciousness

Additional Principles

The following views have been drawn from general life experience. Like any conclusions based on personal opinion, they are open to challenge, but, collectively, I believe, they represent a solid basis on which to build a happy and productive life.

Subjectivity

All experience is subjective. We can only know that which has become apparent to us through the operation of our senses and cogitations. The truth is what we perceive to be true – it is not a monolithic external artefact that remains unavoidable and unchanged for eternity. Even if there were a form of objective and inviolable truth, we could only perceive it through the veil of our own cognitive biases. Such perception would be a personal interpretation, not a comprehensive grasp of this unchanging body of knowledge.

Meaning/purpose

Meaning and purpose are created by the individual. There is no force or entity "out there" which has a plan for the universe or any of its inhabitants.

Life path

People are often encouraged by mentors, whether they be coaches, parents, or pastors, to seek a vocation or life path which will lead to a climactic conclusion, in which the reasons for their success or lack of it will become clear. However, in actuality, life is inevitably a random process – one never knows where one will end up.

Religious philosophies can be divided into two categories regarding the way they conceive the life path:

- Linear: Creation, development, decline, and extirpation follow a timeline determined by the will of an omnipotent creator.
- Cyclic: All events form part of a cyclic progression, which is capable of perpetual repetition and which may have no beginning or conclusion, and is not necessarily under the guidance of a superior being.

Non-expert living assumes that life is a cyclic phenomenon.

Dynamics of existence

A concept that is intertwined with the linear view of the life path is what I have chosen to define as a "peroration." This is a climactic point at which the following events will occur:

- The person will gain knowledge of all the events of their life and their significance;
- The person will be judged and their life experience evaluated;
- The person will be consigned to an eternal existence in either a place of bliss or torment, depending on the result of the judgment;
- This event will occur once and its results will be comprehensive and permanent.

Peroration-style thinking is also often applied to events during a person's lifetime. Many occurrences are described as life-changing or representative of an irrevocable change in personal or public history. The extreme version of this is catastrophism, in which it is held that a cataclysmic event has occurred or is impending which will result in a permanent and disastrous change in society.

Such views and attitudes are antithetical to effective and productive personal functioning. Hoarding one's possessions or obsessively planning strategies to deal with some expected catastrophic event can have two very damaging consequences:

- It limits a person's ability to deal with such difficult events should they occur;
- It creates a negative view of life, people, and the possibilities of the future.

On the other hand, viewing life as a cyclic process can be invigorating and inspiring. There is the well-known fable of the farmer who had a truly phlegmatic approach to life.

This farmer had a valuable horse that ran away one day.
The neighbours said: "Poor man! What a disaster!"
The farmer responded: "Who knows what tomorrow will bring?"
The next day the horse returned, bringing with it a team of wild horses.
The neighbours cried out: "What a great piece of luck!"
The farmer responded: "Who knows what tomorrow will bring?"
The next day, while the farmer's son was breaking in one of the wild horses, it lashed out and broke the boy's leg.
The neighbours expressed their commiserations, and the farmer issued his customary response.
The next day, officers from the army called in search of young men to recruit. Although the farmer's son was exactly the kind of recruit they were seeking, his broken leg rendered him unfit for service.
Again, the neighbours showered the farmer with congratulations, and the farmer continued to preserve his typical nonchalance.

Destination

Where will we all end up?

It is reasonable to accept that no one really knows. As Omar Khayyam wrote in his celebrated Rubaiyat (translation by Edward Fitzgerald):

The Art of Non-Expert Living – Oberon Michaels

Strange, is it not? that of the myriads who
Before us pass'd the door of Darkness through,
Not one returns to tell us of the Road,
Which to discover we must travel too.

The Revelations of Devout and Learn'd
Who rose before us, and as Prophets burn'd,
Are all but Stories, which, awoke from Sleep,
They told their comrades, and to Sleep return'd.

The universe exhibits an apparent continuity, but the nature and timing of changes in the future are essentially matters of speculation. However, the least likely possibility is that humans will be finally locked into an eternal state of psychological stasis. It is possible that there are dimensions and beings whose existence and activity we are currently unaware of, and that we may develop an awareness of such in the future. However, the present is the only temporal space in which we can move, act and plan. The path to reconciliation with the past, and to understanding the future, is by thoroughly, assertively, and joyfully exploring the Now.

Expertise

The Cambridge English Dictionary defines an expert as:

A person with a high level of knowledge or skill relating to a particular subject or activity

So, in practical matters, expertise has two components: knowledge and skill. For example, n the case of a professional discipline like surgery, one would expect the expert practitioner to demonstrate deep knowledge of anatomy and physiology; knowledge of surgical protocols; and an ability to execute surgical procedures skillfully. In the context of academic pursuits, the expert would be expected to show an accurate and detailed knowledge of the subject area; a thorough knowledge of the sources of his/her information; and an ability to demonstrate and explain his knowledge to a non-expert listener.

Many fields of study are built on large bodies of commonly accepted knowledge. Electrical engineers do not argue whether the equations of James Clerk-Maxwell are correct, physicists do not wrangle over the validity of the theory of gravity and historians do not challenge the reality of the dropping of the atomic bomb on Hiroshima in August 1945. While there may be dispute about the application of such knowledge, the basic building blocks of information are accepted as correct.

The two exceptions are philosophy and theology. Philosophy is by nature speculative and explores the infinite range of possible thoughts about the structure of reality and modes of behaviour. Hence, the knowledge derived from philosophical inquiry is always open to continued speculation and investigation.

On the other hand, certain streams of theology purport to represent definite and unvarying knowledge, along with the right to regulate behaviour. For example, the Catholic Church has proclaimed theology to be the "queen of the sciences," suggesting that its conclusions can be checked and verified like those relating to the material sciences.

Therefore, the professional theologian should be expected to demonstrate detailed and specific subject knowledge; communication skills; an ability to interpret the will of God; and the right to regulate people's behaviour. Consider the following example. You decide to go on a lengthy vacation overseas. For advice and assistance in planning the trip, you visit the local travel agent. You are greeted by a young consultant and invited to sit down. The consultant is well-spoken and well presented, and very attentive to your inquiry. In the course of the conversation, you discover that the young man lives a very sheltered life: he lives locally and takes the bus to work, he has no driver's licence, he has never visited an airport or seen a plane close up, he has never been to the seaside, he has never been on a boat, and his great hobby is stamp collecting. One could wonder why a person who has never traveled could be in a position to give travel advice. However, he demonstrates a thorough knowledge of the agency's products and can back all his suggestions with appropriate documentation.

Compare the qualifications of our hypothetical consultant with those of the typical theologian. The knowledge retailed by the young travel agent can be verified by a wide range of documentary sources, which have been verified by travelers to various destinations. What is notable about these sources is their abundance and consistency. Pictures of major tourist attractions like the Pyramids the Statue of Liberty and the

Sydney Harbour Bridge are so common that they can be recognized at a glance. By contrast, the theologian often preaches about a realm of the afterlife, the evidence for which is at the best sketchy, and the documentary support for which is scripture and the garish visions of saints and seers, and reports of near-death experiences. The reliability of the last named has been questioned by skeptics for a number of reasons:

- A significant number of those who return from the near-death state do not report any vision of an afterlife;
- The nature of the afterlife seems to be influenced strongly by the cultural and religious orientation of the subject – Christians see Jesus, Hindus see Krishna, etc
- Neuroscientists have suggested that such visions represent an explosion of electrical activity in the brain

The theologian urges people to worship a deity who is said to have the conflicting attributes of omniscience and omnipotence, and who does not communicate in an obvious way with his creation. Christian scripture states that God reveals himself in two ways:

- Through the majesty and order of his creation (Romans Chapter 1, verses 19 – 20):
  Because that which may be known of God is manifest in them; for God hath shewed it unto them.
  For the invisible things of him from the creation of the world are clearly seen, being understood by the

> *things that are made, even his eternal power and Godhead; so that they are without excuse:*

- Through personal revelation (1 Corinthians, Chapter 2, Verses 12 – 14)
  Now we have received, not the spirit of the world, but the spirit which is of God; that we might know the things that are freely given to us of God.
  Which things also we speak, not in the words which man's wisdom teacheth, but which the Holy Ghost teacheth; comparing spiritual things with spiritual. But the natural man receiveth not the things of the Spirit of God: for they are foolishness unto him: neither can he know them, because they are spiritually discerned.

Hence, both these sources of knowledge are based on a presupposition that a certain powerful and non-physical entity, which cannot be discerned through any sensory mechanism, wishes to make itself known to people and regulate their behaviour.

God is said to be infinite and absolute in his command of reality, but still feels particular wants and makes plans to satisfy those wants. The intentions and wishes of this elusive deity, and its prescriptions for living a worthy life, have been the source of unending and often violent argument since the dawn of organized religion. In many religions, the prime object of the devotee is to gain a favourable position in the afterlife and to regulate his beliefs and behaviours to support this end. The widespread abandonment of Christianity in the developed world can be attributed to the waning of the public belief in a prescriptive after-death state. If there is no Hell, death is much less intimidating.

On the subject of expertise, let us consider another example: You have trained diligently with your football team to master a particular maneuver. The coach is delighted with your dedication and impressed with your skill level and selects you for the next game. In the middle of the game, as you are streaming down the field with the opposition in hapless pursuit, you stop and shout to the coach's box: "Hey coach, am I doing this move right?" The consequences are obvious: the opposition players would catch up with you and dispossess you of the ball, and your team members would be very angry. If, after the game, you offered the following lame excuse to the furious coach: "I just wanted to make sure that I was making the right move," you can imagine what response you would receive.

The truth is that in the moment of action, no one is an expert: the judgement of skill and success comes after the event. Your skill level will be demonstrated in your actions, but those actions are generally the result of training, not of deliberate choice. Therefore, you can train by breaking up and practicing aspects of an activity, but an actual performance is a singular event.

Furthermore, an expert can guide and advise, but you have to do the job yourself. Therefore you should be judicious in your selection of experts. Pick those who you are confident will possess the skills and knowledge to set you on the right track. Your life is a path of self-expression, and it is wise to seek the support of those who can aid you in achieving your worthiest goals.

The Art of Non-Expert Living – Oberon Michaels

Chapter 1: Buddhist Theory

Essential Buddhist Principles

Buddhism has a vast canon that categorizes the foundational elements of existence, as well as establishing/categorizing philosophical and moral principles. However, as my purpose is to empower people to live a happy, purposeful and peaceful life, I have chosen to focus on four aspects that relate most directly to daily life.

- Existence – The Three Signs of Being
- Suffering – The Three Fires
- Personality – The Five Skandhas
- Liberation – The Four Noble Truths

These four categories are universal – they apply to all people, whether religious or not.

The other categories in Buddhist religious theory include the qualities of wisdom; the varieties of temptation; the traits of the ideal practitioner; corrective meditations; and the regions and occupants of the afterlife. In other words, they deal with issues relating specifically to the Buddhist devotee. While these principles may be admirable in themselves, they do not form part of the *Non-Expert Living* curriculum.

As Buddhism developed into an organized religion, first in India, and later in China, Japan, and Korea, Gautama was raised to the status of a deity. When monastic orders were formed, such as those still operating in Japan and Thailand, monks had to swear the following vow:

I take refuge in the Buddha
I take refuge in the Dharma
I take refuge in the Sanga

In this case, the *Buddha* is the divine incarnation known on earth as Gautama; the *Dharma* is the Buddhist doctrine; the *Sanga* is the monastic order. Thus, formal worship became an integral part of religious practice, and just as Buddha became God, the seeker became a devotee.

As time went on, the study of Buddhism became more heavily theological, and the Buddha himself, from being just a sage, became a trinitarian abstraction comprised of the following elements:

- Dharmakaya – the "truth body" or the Buddha in an unmanifested state
- Saṃbhogakāya – the subtle extra-physical body of the Buddha
- Nirmāṇakāya – the "mind-made" body, with which the Buddha could appear in the phenomenal world

Buddhist theology, like that of Christianity, is the plaything of religious philosophers and has little bearing on daily life – except for theologians who derive their income from teaching it.

A wise person eats the fruit that nourishes and avoids that which causes indigestion. My hope is that this book will provide psychological nourishment and help to dispel confusion.

The Three Signs of Being

The Three Signs of Being may be conceived as forming the ontological physics of Buddhism – the nature and indication of *what is*. This arrangement of components accords with many scientific observations and aspects of non-deterministic philosophy, but inevitably clashes with most forms of theology.

Impermanence

This sign has two vital aspects:

- Continuous change
- Inevitable extinction

Nothing is fixed in nature. All things change, even if the rate of change may be imperceptible. The movement of ocean waves will erode the largest and hardest rocks; all animals – including we apes – experience aging and death; even the prodigious production of energy in our Sun will eventually run out, and our nearest star will expire. If we spend an hour with a friend, we do not expect to notice that he or she has aged since the beginning of the meeting; however, if we catch up with this friend after not having had any contact for twenty years, we would expect to observe the effects of aging.

Much philosophy and religion favour the supposition of some permanent and unchanging state of being. As absolute stability does not apply to life on this globe, which is racked by natural cataclysms like earthquakes, volcanoes, tsunamis, and epidemics of disease, and in which physical death is inevitable, theologians like to assert that after death, people will continue to exist for eternity in a fixed and unvarying state in a non-physical dimension.

In some Eastern philosophies it is proposed that the cosmos consists of two dimensions:

- The spirit which is eternal and without form
- The material world which is governed by time and space

Unlike Judeo-Christian religions, Buddhism examines the concept of the Void in great detail. This is the infinite repository of potential from which all material things arise and into which they are later absorbed. In non-religious terms, the void can be equated with the Nothing (of which theoretical physicist Laurence Krauss speaks) which is not "nothing" in the conventional sense, but rather is a sea of boiling energy. In the Book of Genesis, God does not create anything from an absolute absence of existence, but rather brings order to a previous inchoate mess. Hence the cosmos can be seen as the operation of a double duality:

- Unmanifested potential or "spirit" which is eternal and complete in its consistency
- Creation, or the world of manifestation, is governed by an internal and inevitable system of dualities – arising/extinction, coming/going, dark/light, birth/death, etc.

If you have a body, two things are certain:

- It will change
- It will expire

Discontent

Discontent or suffering – sometimes rendered as misery – is one of the most misunderstood concepts in Buddhism. Buddhists are often charged with seeking a joyless and passionless state of equilibrium so that any loss of felicity or arising of pain and suffering can be obviated, or reduced to a bland and unchallenging acceptance. In fact, this could not be further from the truth.

A more elaborate description of this sign is as follows:

> *Wedded to the unloved*
> *Separated from the loved*

The true nature of this sign is the inevitable operation of personal ambition, which provides direction, drive, and excitement, even in the most apparently humdrum life. Rather than misery, it is better defined as divine discontent, which inspires humans to develop rare and wonderful skills, to climb mountains, to investigate the marvelous complexities of nature, and to pursue noble humanitarian goals. Humans do not "do satisfaction" well – we very easily become bored. Nor are we troubled by the fact that we have continually recurring needs: I have never heard of anyone complaining of the troublesome need to keep breathing, the requirement for continuous nutriment, or the body's need for regular sleep. Real suffering is caused by the deprivation of the opportunity to satisfy those needs, as is experienced by the victims of famine, epidemic disease, or extreme poverty.

This constructive discontent is one of the major epistemic problems with popular conceptions of an afterlife. In the article on Hell in the Catholic Encyclopedia (1913), it says:

Many admit the existence of Hell, but deny the eternity of its punishment. (However) Holy Writ is quite explicit in teaching the eternity of the pains of Hell. The torments of the damned shall last forever. They are everlasting just as are the joys of Heaven.

However, if suffering in Hell is eternal and unchanging, it seems reasonable to suppose that the damned soul could eventually accept it as the status quo and come to tolerate it. Therefore, it would cease to be perceived as punishment. Following this line of argument, one could propose a similar problem with the concept of Heaven. The eternal felicity could become commonplace, and the ecstasy of divine communion quite humdrum.

A similar case can be observed in the natural world. The weight of the atmosphere on the human frame is about 14 pounds per square inch, a load that is readily tolerated by even the most feeble of human beings. In extremely sultry conditions, people may feel oppressed by the increase in atmospheric weight due to the higher moisture content in the air, but they don't seek to take the weight of the air off their shoulders. Astronauts living in space for extended periods experience a loss in bone density and can find returning to life in Earth's atmosphere challenging. This constant pressure is necessary for the healthy maintenance of muscle mass, but we do not notice it because we are habituated to it; we know no other condition (unless we are astronauts).

Another interesting example of the necessity for continuous change is human vision. People speak of 'fixing the gaze' on an object. However, this is technically impossible. If the image were held statically on the retina, it would fade away. For effective vision, the eye has to focus and refocus continually on the objects in its environment. Again, in the normal course of events, we don't complain of our eyes getting tired because of this continuous muscular activity, although we may feel the impact of it after a long day of focused work at the computer.

In other words, humans adapt to persistent adverse conditions and often learn to see them as unproblematic. On the other hand, extreme and short-lasting changes, such as violent eruptions of illness or cataclysmic natural disasters, are inevitably a true challenge to humanity's natural tendency for adaptation and create fear and uncertainty. This is the psychology behind torture.

Hence this so-called "sign of misery" can in fact be a real source of achievement and joy, as well as a source of disappointment and suffering. If things ain't changin', we humans just aren't interested. By nature, we are risk takers – we regularly indulge in the thrill caused by incertitude. For example, we usually define a good football game as one where the teams are well-matched and the result remains in doubt until the very end. By comparison, a game in which one of the teams quickly establishes a devastating superiority and maintains it for the entire game is usually judged as being tedious and uninteresting. A preponderance of such unbalanced games would be highly undesirable for the association or league in which teams were competing.

The persistence of the awareness of misery is dependent on memory. Anesthetists, who are acknowledged experts in assessing levels of consciousness, distinguish between several levels of awareness:

- Death – the complete and permanent cessation of all bodily functions;
- Deep unconsciousness – all automatic bodily functions are maintained but the patient has no awareness of his environment and what is taking place in it;
- Sedation – the patient has awareness but no capacity to make memories;
- Full awareness – the patient is fully cognizant of his surroundings and bodily sensations, and has clear recall of his experience.

Hence, if you can't remember it, it won't upset you.

In Zen training, masters encouraged a vigorous acceptance of unavoidable unpleasant aspects of life, as is illustrated in the following dialogue.

Student: Why are Zen monasteries located in such inhospitable locations? In winter, we almost freeze to death, and in the summer the weather is unbearably sultry and we are attacked unremittingly by the mosquitos.
Master: There is an easy solution to this problem.
Student: What is that, sir?
Master: Move to a place where the winters are temperate, the summers are pleasant and there are no mosquitos.
Student: But where can one find such a place?
Master: In winter, the master almost freezes to death, the summers are unbearably sultry and he is attacked unremittingly by the mosquitos.

Here the master is, among other things, attacking the assumption that a person will be able to achieve his goals more readily if all sources of discomfort and discouragement are removed. The master is pointing out that an essential part of Zen training is making use of such difficulties as a productive source of discipline. And removing them would be of no advantage to the student.

Lack of Self-identity

One of the popular preoccupations of psychology is "finding oneself." We are encouraged to believe that each of us has a unique and essential core, which is unchanging and which will persist after the death of the body, and possibly for eternity. In religious parlance, this entity is defined as the "soul" and is the driver and decision maker in relation to the body, filling a similar role to the driver of a vehicle. The destruction of the vehicle may not necessarily entail the destruction of the driver.

Classic Buddhist philosophy has no place for what it sees as a superfluous entity, whether it be defined as a self, a psyche, or a soul. A human being is a complex entity, composed of a vast assemblage of components, which must operate harmoniously for the human to survive and thrive. As I will explain in the section on the Five Skandhas, the development of the human is a process of emergence rather than creation.

Traditional Zen training sought vigorously to discourage this narcissistic view of a self, as is demonstrated in this dialogue.

Student: I feel frustrated; I am unable to find my true self.

Master: If you found a self what would you do with it?

Complexity in an entity often has the effect of creating a sense of structural integrity. It is tempting to assume that a complex and substantial structure has an irreducible core, a "foundation stone" on which the superstructure rests, an essential "something" not susceptible to further reduction. For human beings, this core has been variously defined as the self or the soul, a pervasive entity that endures all external fluctuations, but which itself is not essentially changed.

The witness of this enduring element is often said to be consciousness, which may be defined as the ability of an entity to perceive itself as being separate from its environment. Hence, consciousness can be conceived as being as eternal, or at least existing before the formation of the body and enduring long past its demise, and hence separate from it. The doctrines of most organized religions require the rejection of the idea that consciousness could be an emergent faculty derived from the concomitant functions of a multiplicity of functions.

This constitutive view of individual consciousness has been thoughtfully explored in contemporary film and fiction. For example, an interesting and relevant supposition underlies the plot of the first full-length Star Trek film, in which a rogue spacecraft, after extensive wandering through the universe, accumulates so much knowledge that it becomes sentient.

Another example is the TV series *Humans*, in which many of the humdrum operations in modern society have been allocated to non-sentient androids. However, the developer of the robots has also built six units that are sentient. What is the key to this anomalous sentience? 17,000 additional lines of code.

An earlier and more chilling exploration of the insubstantiality of personal identity is the short story *Exit*, by Harry Farjeon. At a Christmas house party, guests have been invited to demonstrate tricks. An elderly and sinister man, Mr Geeles, claims not only to be able to cancel the existence of a random person, but also to completely expunge the record of that person from all human memory. Although he succeeds in meeting this challenge, he is unable to prove his success, as none of the other guests retain a memory of the vanished person.

It is natural that people are attracted by the thought that their experiences form part of a firm history and display an enduring concreteness. All that happens to us appears so real and significant that we are persuaded that our status as witnesses of this amazing panoply of events indicates the endurance of consciousness beyond the demise of the physical body. Most organized religions encourage this view, and offer strategies to ensure that their subscribers will qualify for the best places in the afterlife.

However, the truth is that all experience is subjective and is the result of the personal interpretation of stimuli from the world around us. The quality of those interpretations is dictated by many factors, most of which are outside of our control, including the following:

- Language
- Social conditioning
- Physical aptitude
- Intellectual aptitude

- Health
- Memories

A couple of examples will illustrate the variability of impressions that witnesses can obtain from the same event.

You are visiting China for the first time, and have no knowledge of the Chinese language. In the major square of a big city, a person who appears to be some kind of official dignitary is standing on a podium and delivering a speech. You notice that many of the onlookers are demonstrating extreme emotional reactions. Of course, you are not moved, because you do not understand what the speaker is saying. Later you ask a bilingual friend to explain what has been said. He may say one of the following about the content of the announcement:

- The government will be making a compulsory acquisition of a great number of houses in the district, which will be demolished to enable the building of a new dam;
- A plane from the city's airport has crashed shortly after takeoff, and all the passengers have been killed;
- A Chinese athlete has just won the Olympic men's Marathon;
- The speaker was reciting a classic piece of Chinese literature.

In the first case, you may feel sympathy for those about to lose their homes and annoyance at the high-handed action of the government. In the second, you may initially feel general sympathy for the bereaved families. Later on, if you realize that one of your close friends from university came from that city, and on further investigation, discover that she has indeed lost her life in the crash, your grief will become much more profound and you may be impelled to reach out to her family with a message of sympathy. Regarding the marathon victory, you have no interest in athletic sports or the Olympics, and therefore the news makes little impact on you. In the last case, you accept your friend's word that the artistic performance was indeed a moving experience for those that understood it, but this piece of information is unlike to make the event more significant for you. None of these scenarios changes was said by the speaker, but your reaction is entirely different depending on your perception of what the speaker has said.

Another example is a football game. Your impressions will depend on your investment in and your knowledge of the game. If you have no interest in and knowledge of the game, you will recognize that it represents some code of football, and will assume that it has rules and a particular method of scoring, and that is the limit of your knowledge. If you have a basic familiarity with the game, you will understand the basic rules and scoring system, and be able to work out if one team is significantly superior. If you have expert knowledge, you will immediately work out the strategies being employed by the coaches, which player is in which position, which player is being marked by the opposition, and the finer points of the interpretation of the rules by the umpire (referee). If you are a player, an official, or a supporter, your view and memory of the event will vary accordingly.

However, the operation and result of the match remain unchanged, regardless of the perceptions of the participants and onlookers.

With the development of information technology, a view has been proposed that information storage and retrieval is a process rather than a search through concrete artefacts of knowledge. Information can be seen as a perception of essential organization of data, an appreciation of a new order: the pile of bricks on the ground has become a wall. When you receive the terrifying message on your computer monitor, "no disk found" and realize that the hard disk has died, you don't try to open the disk enclosure and look for all those images, spreadsheets, text files, and videos that were stored on the disk; you accept that the irretrievable perturbation of the bits and bytes has resulted in the destruction of the information.

In the world of nature, we accept that certain manifestations will cease when a process is terminated. When a candle burns down and becomes extinguished, we don't wonder where the fire has gone – we realize that the disappearance of the fire means that the process of combustion has ceased. Similarly, with our mental processes, once the firing of neurons has ceased, there are no memories, no calculations, and no responses, and there are no chunks of information that can be dug out of the brain.

Thus, when you leave the body, it appears that the engine of consciousness which maintains a personal record of events ceases to function permanently, and the memories are expunged as thoroughly as the party guest in Harry Farjeon's story. However, whether records of events are retained in some larger generic dimension of consciousness is open to question.

For example, a theory of morphic resonance has been developed by biologist Rupert Sheldrake, according to which memories are not stored in the brain but in a field; access to that information is achieved by attunement to the field. While the theory is controversial, it does offer an attractive explanation of the apparent non-locality of information and the genetic inheritance of learning.

We are purpose-seeking beings. We are attracted by the belief that our lives have objective meaning (which is derived from a sense of purpose) and that a greater purpose governs the operation of the Universe. We then deduce that the cosmos is governed by a being who has an overarching purpose, which embraces the creation, maintenance, and dissolution of all things.

Many Christian theologians claim that their beliefs represent absolute truth, and that non-theists are inevitably mired in a morass of relativism. In his last address as prefect of the Congregation for the Doctrine of the Faith (formerly the Roman and Universal Inquisition), Cardinal Josef Ratzinger, before his elevation as Pope Benedict XVI, warned of a "dictatorship of relativism" that he claimed was threatening organized religion and corrupting moral sensibilities across the globe. The future pontiff was particularly distressed at the idea of people making up their own minds about moral and cultural issues without the guidance of ecclesiastical authorities.

A similar warning can be heard echoing through the sermons of Protestant preachers who stand upon a conception of 'absolute truth'. It should be noted that Ratzinger's curious statement does not make it clear whether this "dictatorship" is an imposition by an external agent (as tyrannies generally are), or whether "relativism" has a commanding power that crushes the possibility of entertaining any opposing thought. The irony is that religious beliefs are derived from subjective experience and that the religious model of cosmic governance and regulation is unavoidably anthropomorphic. Man has fashioned the divinity that he worships, and the dogmas so energetically preached in churches and seminaries are derived from the intellectual prejudices of clergy and shaped by the forces of political necessity.

At its highest level, religion can be seen as an effort to link individual consciousness with a consciousness that is universal. At the end of his controversial "synoptic" history of mankind, *The Martyrdom of Man*, Winwood Reade (who was accused of being an atheist) presents a theory that the entire cosmos is evolving as a unified system and that human development is an inevitable part of this continuum. Hindu and classic Buddhist philosophy propose that there is a supernal reality, a state of total 'beyondness', surrounding and permeating the basket of the phenomenal world—and that it is possible to attain awareness of this reality. As comedian Woody Allen quipped, "Eternal Nothingness is OK if you are dressed for it." According to Buddhist philosophy, the "costume" of the Five Skandhas is not the right form of dress.

Experience suggests that you can know *what* you have done, but not really *who* you are.

History usually defines people, not by describing their internal state, but by recording their actions and judging them accordingly. The record of the action may remain, but the perceptions of the actor vanish.

Summary

The Three Signs – impermanence, discontent, and lack of self-identity - are of a piece – each of them represents a validation of the other two.

Impermanence breeds discontent and makes the establishment of a permanent and invariable self impossible.

Discontent is driven by a desire for stability that prevents the perceived self from resting comfortably in an established sense of identity.

Lack of self-identity drives us to seek some fixed point of self-recognition in a constantly changing and imperfect world.

The wisest course to learn to ride the continuous currents of change as a surfer rides the ocean wave. We cannot change the wave, but we can learn to harmonize with it. When the wave crashes onto the shore it ceases to be: but we, in the short time allowed can return to seek another wave.

The Three Fires

According to Buddhist philosophy, suffering is generated from three primary sources which are characterized as the Three Fires:

- Attraction (greed)
- Aversion (hate)
- Ignorance (delusion)

The origin of the doctrine of the Three Fires is traditionally believed to be the Fire Sermon, the third public address given by the Buddha after he attained enlightenment. He proposed that all creation is on fire, including the sources of human sensation. Eventually, the devout disciple grows weary of the constant stimulation of the senses, and when the fire dies down, desire fades with it. The disciple loosens the shackles which keep him confined in Samsara, or the world of manifestation, and escapes from his state of conditioned existence.

Fire provides heat, and without heat, there can be no life. Fire also consumes and, when it does so, all it leaves is ashes. The eventual end of our universe will be heat death – the absolute absence of fire. Hence, fire is both essential and destructive. Therefore, in our life journey, we must learn to use fire to light our way and to provide energy, while avoiding being consumed by greed or dazzled by superficial brilliance.

Attraction and aversion are the two sides of the Second Sign of Being: Misery or Discontent. In the picturesque words of Buddhist scripture:

Separated from the Loved
Wedded to the Unloved

Neither of these two fires is intrinsically good or bad: they become beneficial or destructive according to the way in which they are used, just as natural fire can be used to cook a meal or to burn down a house.

Ignorance is the clouding of the intellect, by which we are led to believe that we can be relieved of suffering by the satisfaction of desire.

Attraction

Certain people and things have the power to draw us to them. The bonds thus formed can strengthen a person by providing support and encouragement, or can weaken a person by luring them into destructive attitudes and practices. One may be attracted to a union with another person which is empowering and productive for both parties. Similarly, one person may tempt another to commit a crime or to develop an unhealthy addictive habit.

Attraction is necessary for the development of complex structures. For instance, our bodies could not have come into being without the cooperative coalescing of substances and organisms. Such is the case also with organizational structures. For example, army personnel are united by a sense of patriotism and compelling purpose.

Aversion

Hatred or aversion commonly leads to one of two results:

- Avoidance
- Confrontation

By instinct, we tend to shy away from unpleasant and intimidating circumstances. The cause of this avoidance may be disgust, fear, or natural prudence. Life becomes dysfunctional when we seek to avoid duties that we are required to perform, and people with which we are required to interact.

When we seek to oppose or overcome an obstacle or a person directly, hostility is usually aroused. Through confrontation, we are trying to overcome the obstacle or force the person into subservience. Obstacles may be removed permanently, but in the case of a person, the negative emotions of contempt on the part of the victor and resentment on the part of the loser may well remain.

There are some forms of aversion which cannot be entirely removed from life. For example, everyone needs to use the bathroom. A well-ordered city contains both beautiful gardens and well-managed – and discreetly located - rubbish dumps.

Ignorance

The usual use of this term denotes lack of knowledge, and in colloquial usage, may describe an inability to behave in a courteous and reasonable manner. However, in this case, it may be better understood as confusion – not really knowing "what is what." Hence it is sometimes rendered as "illusion."

The confusion is brought about by our lack of knowledge of our true nature. We don't know who we really are, and consequently, our purposes are ill-formed and our choices ill-judged. Even though we are in the heat of battle, we do not understand who the enemy really is.

The Fire which does not consume

Possibly the most famous image of a fire that burns without destroying that which is on fire is the burning bush [Exodus 2:3]:

And the angel of the Lord appeared unto him in a flame of fire out of the midst of a bush: and he looked, and, behold, the bush burned with fire, and the bush was not consumed.

In the Islamic afterworld, Hell or Jahannam is a raging pit of fire in which all sinners are immersed. The heinous the sin the deeper the level to which the damned soul sinks.

In the Inferno, Dante also describes several categories of sinners who are punished by permanent contact with fire. In the Sixth Circle heretics are confined in burning tombs. Lower down, in the Eighth Circle, which is divided into ten trenches, various types of practitioners of fraud are punished. In the third trench simoniacs (those who trade in ecclesiastical favors and objects) are wedged upside down in holes in the rock while tongues of flame play on the soles of their feet. One of these sinners is Pope Nicholas III. In the tenth trench, counselors of evil and falsehood, one of whom is Ulysses. wander about wrapped in individual flames.

In the Buddhist view, this purgative fire is located in the phenomenal world. In the Fire Sermon (The Third Discourse of the Buddha - Ādittapariyāya Sutta in Pali), the Buddha states that everything in creation is on fire. As with the fire which is said to characterize the infernal afterworld of Christianity and Islam, such a blaze cannot be extinguished – it has to be endured.

The Three Fires of Buddhist doctrine can be seen as modes of expression of the Second Sign of Being – Discontent/Misery.

Coping with the heat

Everyone is familiar with the maxim: "If you can't stand the heat, get out of the kitchen. However, the only release from the cauldron of life is death. So, the best approach is for us to channel the heat of desire to enable us to achieve worthy and satisfying goals and endeavours that will inspire and entertain our fellow sufferers.

The Five Skandhas

How is the human being constituted?

The one component of the human organism which is immediately apparent is the body. In general information about the structure of the body (anatomy) and its various functions (physiology) are widely accepted.

However, there are aspects of embodied life that cause great and ongoing contention. These include how the body is animated, how the process of thinking occurs, and whether and how non-physical entities are associated with the body.

A prime source of disagreement is mind-body dualism. Is the body a machine that is driven and maintained by an immaterial mind? Or is the mind a constituent of the physical body? Are there multiple non-physical entities associated with each body?

Christianity and Islam

Many Christians and Muslims assert that human beings have a soul and a body. In Islam, and a large number of Christian denominations, the body is said to endure for a single lifetime —after which it is subject to a divine judgement and consigned to heaven or hell for all eternity. At the end of time, the bodies of the dead will be resurrected and joined back to their souls, thus amplifying the bliss of the saved and the torment of the damned.

Some Christian denominations do not propound a physical resurrection though, and simply focus on what happens to the 'eternal spirit' or soul of a believer.

Naturally, one of the prime functions of these denominations is to ensure that their subscribers make it to heaven. Various strategies and practices are prescribed so that salvation can be assured.

Hinduism

Hindu philosophy proposes that there are four essential elements to a human being:

- The physical body
- The astral body
- The causal body
- The soul

The soul is considered to be the enduring core of a person, and the three bodies are coverings or garments which overlap each other. The physical body is the coarsest and shortest-lived, the astral body is finer and much longer lived, and the causal body is the finest of the three and can endure for thousands of years. The path of liberation, by which one progressively sheds the three bodies and realizes one's essential identity as a spotless soul is necessarily a very lengthy process and requires multiple reincarnations.

Buddhism

The Buddha subscribed to the principles of reincarnation and liberation but strove to dispel the practice of devotees buying their way into heaven through ritual. The plain and severe message of the original Buddhist doctrine was that the path to liberation involved becoming aware of one's true nature. Accordingly, a special view of the constituents of human beings was developed, and these have been defined as the five aggregates or *skandhas*:

- Form
- Sensation
- Perception
- Tendency
- Consciousness

Form

All living things in the material world possess a body. If there is nobody there is no capacity for movement, thought, awareness, or personal identity. In religious art, even divine beings are usually represented a humanoid form and evil beings by images that are distortions of human or animal forms.

Sensation

This connotes the information received from the senses: images, sounds, tactile impressions, tastes and flavours, and odours. This is data in raw form.

Perception

Perceptions are the mental constructions formed from sensory input. Collectively, they form the interpretations which constitute a person's worldview. For each person, the world is as he or she sees it.

Tendencies

In Buddhist and Hindu philosophy, these are sometimes called *karmic tendencies*, or emotional predispositions carried from incarnation to incarnation. They represent the prime drivers in a person's emotional makeup. For example, some may have a pronounced inclination towards fear, others towards anger, yet others towards ease and sloth. Studies in neurology and pharmacology have indicated that many persistent emotional states have their origin in body chemistry, diet, and consumption of pharmaceuticals (legal and illegal.)

Consciousness

This is the faculty by which we perceive ourselves as separate entities and independent actors in our environment. In many ways, consciousness is the final frontier in neurological research and, according to some, the last protective wall to fall in the citadel of organized religion.

All animals exhibit consciousness to some degree. Predators are aware of their prey and where it can be found, and prey is aware of its vulnerability and strategies for escape and concealment. However, there is a development of consciousness which we may call *sentience*, in which one becomes cognizant of possessing a unique and distinct identity. For example, a dog can learn its own name and develop specific behaviours regarding the people it lives with. The most advanced state of sentience is exhibited by human beings, to whose awareness of personal identity is added the capacity to make a wide range of choices. Whether these choices are actually made freely is a subject of intense discussion among philosophers and medical scientists, but in any case, the appearance of choice is commonly accepted by most people.

For a human being to be considered operational, all five *skandhas* must be functional.

In the ultimate state of awareness, the object, the observer, and the act of observation collapse into a unified state of "*is-ness*," which resides outside the bounds of time and space.

The Four Noble Truths

The first sermon preached by Gautama Buddha after attaining enlightenment was recorded in the *Dharmacakrapravartana Sūtra*, or the *Setting in Motion of the Wheel of the Dharma Sutra*. It contains the seminal doctrine of Buddhism – the Four Noble Truths -, which addresses the issue of human suffering and the appropriate method for dealing with it.

The cause of suffering, and the ways in which release from suffering can be attained, are summarized in the Four Noble Truths:

>Truth 1: Man is in a continual state of suffering.

>Truth 2: The cause of suffering is unsatisfied desire.

>Truth 3: Man can escape suffering through the cessation or extirpation of desire.

>Truth 4: The way to permanent relief from suffering is the Noble Eightfold Path:

>(1) Right Understanding

>(2) Right Intention

>(3) Right Speech

>(4) Right Conduct

>(5) Right Livelihood

>(6) Right Effort

>(7) Right Thought

>(8) Right Meditation

Suffering is most clearly associated with the second *Sign of Being*: Misery or Discontent. Human beings will never be happy through the satisfaction of personal desire because, due to the instability of the human condition, the generation of desire is endless. What the Buddhist aims at is not the crushing of desires – because the wish to avoid desire would also be a desire – but a state of reconciliation in which his being is not *trapped* or defined by desire.

The term "right" specified in the steps of the Noble Eightfold refers to that which is most effective, or most appropriate, rather than to something that is 'correct' in a constructed moral sense. The path represents the height of moral pragmatism, not a tortuous track through an obstacle course of evils to a destination of divine stasis.

Successful traversal of the path does not involve "victory" over an external enemy like the Devil, but rather requires self-conquest – the liberating self-knowledge that can be construed in Jesus' statement, "The truth shall make you free" (John 8:32). Christian preachers usually interpret Christ's words as an imperative to the absorption of religious dogma ("the truth"), rather (and more fruitfully) than as a reference to perceptions of reality that are obscured by delusions of selfhood.

The Path

The path can be divided into three steps or phases:

1. Mental preparation: right understanding, right intention
2. Practical application: right speech, right conduct, right livelihood, right effort
3. Realization: right thought, right meditation.

However, these should not be conceived of as a sequence in which the practice of earlier steps is abandoned when the aspirant reaches a later step. The truly realized being will practice all steps concurrently.

The Art of Non-Expert Living – Oberon Michaels

Chapter 2: The Buddhist Background

Buddhism: An Outline

According to Wikipedia, in 2020, Buddhism was the world's fourth largest religion in terms of the number of followers:

- Christianity - 2.38 billion
- Islam - 1.91 billion
- Hinduism - 1.16 billion
- Buddhism - 507 million

The founder and leading figure of Buddhism was Siddartha Gautama, an Indian prince who was born in Lumbini, in modern-day Nepal. The dates of his life are uncertain but mainstream scholarship generally agrees that he lived for about eighty years spanning the sixth and fifth centuries BCE.

The legend tells that, before Gautama's birth, his father received a prophecy that the boy would quit royal life and become a mendicant. To forestall this unappealing eventuality, the father took all possible steps to guard the youth against the ugliness of the outside world. Gautama, who grew into a very handsome and charming young man, was kept in an environment of extreme luxury and was prevented from witnessing anything unpleasant. As part of his royal duty, he married a beautiful and upright princess. The couple had just welcomed their first child when one day, Gautama summoned his charioteer and took a drive into the countryside, far beyond the bounds of the palace estate. For the first time in his life, he caught sight of four things that radically changed his worldview: a very sick man; a very old man; a corpse; and a meditating sage.

The faithful charioteer explained that sickness, ageing, and death were unavoidable aspects of life and that the sage was seeking to escape the limitations of phenomenal existence by the practice of meditation.

Gautama was inspired to seek the ultimate truth behind the fluctuations of worldly life, and came to an abrupt decision: he would leave his wife, child, and life of princely entitlement and seek wisdom through rigorous spiritual practices. Retreating to the forest, he became a radical ascetic, arousing admiration among his fellow seekers by the severity of his personal discipline. However, reduced to a shadow and close to dying, he realized that his asceticism had not brought him the understanding he was seeking. It now became clear to him that disciplined moderation was required for the spiritual search, and he abandoned his ascetic practices. His followers assumed that he had failed in his spiritual ambitions and most of them quit his company in disgust. Undaunted, Gautama continued his routine of intense introspection, and one day, when seated under a Bo (pipal) tree, final illumination came to him. He realized the insubstantiality of all forms and the futility of all ritual, and understood that humanity's major problem is the suffering caused by incessant desire.

In the **Deer Park in Sarnat**, Gautama is said to have met five of his former disciples and converted them to his new doctrine of the Middle Way – a lifestyle marked by sensible moderation, meditation, observance of moral principles, and compassionate interaction with all sentient beings. Gautama continued to support many of the doctrines inherited from his Hindu background, most notably reincarnation. However, his dismissal of ritual and the prerogatives of the Hindu priesthood aroused considerable opposition, and eventually led to the effective expulsion of Buddhism from India several centuries later. By this time, the religion had spread to China and surrounding Asian countries. In the Fourth Century CE, it spread to Korea and two centuries later to Japan, which is today one of the strongholds of the religion. Due to the efforts of European scholars, Buddhist literature began to be distributed in the West in the nineteenth century, and while the religion itself has not gained a vast number of converts outside Asia, Buddhist thought has had a profound effect on European philosophy and literature.

As with most other religions, Buddhism developed its own hagiography and eschatology, reflecting the influence of Hinduism. From just a sage, Gautama evolved into a miracle worker and divine being, one in a long series of Buddhas. Before his enlightenment, he was said to have been accosted by the devil, who was making a last-ditch effort to block Gautama's road to spiritual illumination. After he attained realization, it is said that he was visited by angelic beings and that the heavens were made glorious by his attainment. The acceptance of the theory of reincarnation led to the speculation on the structure and population of extra-physical realms, and Buddhist eschatology (theory of the afterlife), like the eschatology of Christianity and Islam, has its own ghoulish infernal regions.

However, despite some garish accretions, Buddhism remains a religion of principle and practice, rather than one of observance and reward. The basic pillars of the faith are accepted by all Buddhist schools, and controversies over fundamental dogmas, which have afflicted the Judeo-Christian religions, have been addressed by intentions to conciliate rather than to fight. A notable demonstration of this collegiality is the success of the eminent British jurist and spokesman for Buddhism, Christmas Humphries (1901 – 1983), in persuading representatives of most major Buddhist sects to endorse his "Twelve Principles of Buddhism."

Principle number 11 commences:

The Buddha said: "Work out your own salvation with diligence". Buddhism knows no authority for truth save the intuition of the individual, and that is authority for himself alone.

Such a view would be anathema in many other religions. For example, Cardinal Josef Ratzinger (later Pope Benedict XVI) raised hackles with controversial statements about Buddhism and Hinduism in a 1997 interview with French magazine *L'Express*. He defined the former as a sort of *"spiritual auto-eroticism [un autoerotisme spirituel]."* He expressed his dislike of a religion which claimed to offer contact with the divine without specific ritual obligations and also referred to a prophecy dating back to the 1950s in which it was said that Buddhism rather than Marxism would be the major challenge to the Church in the Twentieth Century.

Later his Eminence clarified that *"autoerotisme spirituel"* would more appropriately be translated as "narcissism," and should not be associated with carnality.

Buddhist sects

Buddhism has evolved into a number of schools, each focusing on a particular path to liberation. These schools can be divided into two major groups:

- *Theravada* or *Hinayana* (lesser vehicle) – practised today in Thailand, Myanmar, Sri Lanka, Laos, and Cambodia
- *Mahayana* (great vehicle) – practised today in China, Mongolia, Hong Kong, Korea, Japan, Singapore, Vietnam, Nepal, Malaysia, Taiwan, and Bhutan.

In the *Theravada* schools, the ideal devotee is the *Arhat* – one who observes moral principles and meditative practices to attain enlightenment. In the *Mahayana*, it is the *Boddhisattva* – one who strives to gain enlightenment not only for himself but for all sentient beings.

One of the best-known schools in the *Mahayana* canon is *Zen*. Much of the material in this book has been drawn from *Zen* literature. However, this is not to suggest that other Buddhist sects are deficient in providing a solid and valuable foundation for living a meaningful and satisfying life. I have found *Zen* appealing because it cuts to the chase: its focus on direct seeing into reality is particularly relevant in the complex and confusing world of today.

Buddhism and other faiths

Because of Buddhism's fundamentally tolerant nature, Buddhists rarely indulge in persecution of other believers. While there are a couple of notable exceptions in which militant Buddhist regimes have indulged in persecution – like the current Junta in Myanmar against the Rohingya, and the Japanese in World War II – the primary emphasis in Buddhist doctrine on compassion is apparent in inter-religious relationships. Buddhists have much more often been the victims of persecution than the generators of it.

Zen: a historical view

Zen can be considered the highest and most direct application of basic Buddhist principles to daily life. While its quirkiness and favouring of unorthodoxy have given it a certain currency in the West, it is important to understand that it forms part of a very long religious tradition and is extremely disciplined in its structure.

Life in Western society has been undergoing a process of compartmentalization since the Renaissance, a development that became more pronounced during the Industrial Revolution and accelerated dramatically during the twentieth century. Nowadays, not only do we consign much of the management of our lives to specialist professionals, such as doctors, lawyers, and clergy, but we also view our own activities as separate and discrete entities. One might attend church services to fulfill religious obligations that seem to cease as soon as one leaves the church. One might study ethics and moral philosophy at university with no expectation that one's behaviour will or should be affected in the process. People watch violent films, and then vigorously deny that such films inspire other people to commit acts of violence. Compartmentalization, useful as a tool in organizing activity, has been elevated to the level of an art, engendering a divorce between thought and deed, between ideal and action. When life is reduced to a series of snapshots, people are encouraged to judge by appearances and to value things for their convenience: an attitude that not only masks the deeper problems of human existence but can render one helpless when facing any situation of crisis.

The recent popularity of Zen is unfortunately related to the tendency for people to value only the aspects of an activity that appeal to them, and to discard the rest. While syncretism is a fundamental element in the development of a religion, a distinction has to be made between the foundational pillars of doctrine and the surface features of religious ritual. One can recall the case of Oscar Wilde who found the gorgeous rituals of Catholic worship very attractive while being unwilling to adhere to the severe Catholic moral teaching. In the West, Zen has been valued for its unabashed quirkiness, its directness, its aggressive non-conformism, and its problem-solving potential. What is often forgotten is that Zen is primarily a religious philosophy, albeit one that emphasizes action rather than speculation. When Zen is regarded as a fashionable novelty, it soon loses its charm and its richness and power are not fully appreciated. It must be understood that Zen is the primer for a well-proven process of personal development – one that requires years of patient and persistent effort to produce results of lasting value. In fact, Zen is nothing less than a set of practices designed to force students to the most acute point of crisis: one that cannot be resolved by any conventional means of palliation. The crises that most of us in the West dread and try to avoid are welcomed by the Zen practitioner: for if you resolve the ultimate crisis, you will enjoy ultimate satisfaction.

The origin of Zen

Zen, it should be remembered, is shorthand for *Zen Buddhism*. The word *Zen* itself is a corruption of the Chinese word cha'an, which is itself a corruption of the Sanskrit term dhyana, meaning contemplation. So even in its name, Zen is something of an affront to religious scholarship that insists upon religious truth as that which is untainted! This "in your face" quality pervades Zen in both its history and practice. Being nothing less than an attempt to bring the student to face reality directly in the most immediate manner, Zen seeks to shock the practitioner out of his complacency and to deprive him of all his psychological props, until there exists nothing between him and the vision of the 'original face', the appearance of absolute identity, the affirmation of a reality perceived with an intensity that goes far beyond mere conviction.

However, for all its iconoclasm, Zen is still a form of Buddhism. Much of the practice of Zen is carried on in monasteries, in which life is strictly regimented according to monastic traditions which are more rigorous than those used in the Western world. Zen monks spend much time reciting the Buddhist sutras and meditating, as do other Buddhist clergy. What distinguishes the earnest student of Zen from his other Buddhist colleagues is the intensity of his search for ultimate subjectivity. He is prepared to give everything to attain what Alan Watts has called the "wisdom of insecurity" – to be at one with whatever happens, totally free of fear or regret. However, to attain this freedom the student must endure precise and exacting discipline. Eccentric, careless or immoral behaviour is discouraged, just as it would be in any other religious institution.

Technically, Zen Buddhism belongs to the tradition of *Mahayana* (Greater Vehicle) Buddhism, so called to distinguish it from the *Hinayana* (Lesser Vehicle) tradition. The broad difference between the two is in the quality sought by the aspirant. In the *Hinayana*, which is the earlier form and which focuses strictly on a canon of early Buddhist texts, the religious ideal is that of the *Arhat*: the person who has achieved a state of liberation in which all desires have been extirpated, and who therefore qualifies for entry into *Nirvana*, the Buddhist heaven. In the *Mahayana*, which is a later development, the ideal is that of the *Bodhisattva*: one who achieves liberation but who, with infinite compassion, bypasses *Nirvana* and returns to work for the salvation of his deluded brethren. The body of *Mahayana* scriptures is vast and, while some texts are considered to be particularly important, none is regarded as canonical.

Mahayana Buddhism is not a single school but rather a collection of Buddhist movements. Zen is one of these offshoots, which has attracted particular attention because of its extreme nature. Zen strives to push the bounds of religious philosophy as far as possible, appearing to become in the process almost free of conventional religious connotations. While many profound treatises have been written by Zen masters, the business of Zen is with the activities and machinery of daily life. Zen is in fact the most anecdotal of religious forms. The intellectual diet of the disciple is stories and reported conversations (*mondo* in Japanese) involving Zen practitioners, rather than the great *sutras* and scriptures. The ultimate development of these philosophical tools is the *koan*: a nonsensical statement or an insoluble conundrum on which the student concentrates until the ratiocinative machinery of the mind grinds to a halt, opening the way for a new view of reality in which all dualities are resolved or redefined in a totally harmonious way.

Dualisms

Religion is humanity's response to the problems caused by the apparently inevitable dualities of life. Everything in the phenomenal world has its opposite, and human history is the record of pendulum swings among an infinite array of pairs of opposing qualities. In its earliest phase, religion was propitiative or invoking: men wanted to be on the right side of the unseen powers governing the universe. Incurring the wrath of nature could lead to disaster or demise in a world where absence signified extinction. As human beings developed civil laws, religion became prescriptive, and to a certain extent, predictive. Systems of morality developed in which certain actions were rewarded with approbation, and sometimes also with material advantages, and other actions drew vengeance from either divine or human agents. In these two stages, religion was trapped in a net of dualities: good and evil, just and unjust, desirable and undesirable, etc. This simple system of duality is still powerful within major religions such as Islam and Christianity today.

The next phase was to challenge dualism as a framework of thought. Among religions, Buddhism most fiercely tackles the problem of duality, and does so in both philosophical and active terms. In Buddhism, a double system of dualities operates:

- duality in the phenomenal world: good/evil etc
- a universal duality consisting of the phenomenal world and the *Void* i.e. that which lies beyond the world of appearances.

The paradoxical, but amazingly satisfying conclusion is that in fact only the Void exists, i.e. is a permanent reality, while the material world, which appears so concrete, is an illusion wrought by a process of continuous change. The Void is the repository of all possibilities and is qualitatively limitless. As soon as something is plucked from the Void and manifests itself as a recognizable form, it is, in a sense, dead: its identity has become frozen with an absolute loss of potential. Hinduism, with its love of complicated mythology, describes the Void as the abode of the divine spirit existing beyond creation. Buddhism and Hinduism agree in viewing the phenomenal world as totally insubstantial and undependable.

Other major religions, where the emphasis is on organizational rather than personal growth, have been unwilling to embrace the concept of double duality. Christianity and Islam are in effect franchisers of religion, discrete organizations, rather than the cultural expression of a religious milieu. In fact, Christianity could be said to be the first franchise in recorded history, a corporate rather than a religious milestone. As the corporate approach to the world spread with the development of sovereign nations and then companies, corporate religious groups imposed more restrictions on the beliefs and lifestyles of their subscribers. In medieval times theologians, the "doctors of the soul" laid down exactly how one was to live, the reward for compliance being a place in Heaven. Non-compliance could lead to severe punishment, both in this world and the next.

People who enjoyed personal religious experiences or higher states of consciousness were often discouraged, if not punished, in their lifetimes. Many victims of religious persecution, of course, have been posthumously rehabilitated and their visions declared genuine. A notable case is that of Joan of Arc, burnt at the stake in 1431, rehabilitated in 1456, and canonized in 1920. Hence, a sincere search for religious truth could be a very dangerous process.

In Christianity and Islam death is seen as the gateway to immortality, the termination of a single life on earth, after which the soul would be raised to an eternal state of bliss, or consigned to a region of unending torment.

In both Buddhism and Hinduism, creation is seen as a dance of death. Whatever is born must die, whatever is young must grow old, and whatever is new will in time become familiar. This realization drove adherents to seek for the ultimate resolution: how to attain a state of pervasive awareness while participating effectively in the inevitable processes of change. More than any other approach, Zen stresses the urgency of this search and uses any device necessary to bring realization to the practitioner as soon as possible. The emphasis is on direct experience as the only path to knowledge: no priests, dogma, or ceremonies can bring realization to anyone.

The beginnings of Zen Buddhism

The history of Zen is considered to have begun with the settling in China of a Buddhist monk, *Bodhidharma*, known as the First Patriarch of Zen, around 520 CE. In contrast to religious reformers such as Buddha and Confucius, little is known of the life of Bodhidharma, but what has come down to us relates entirely to his practice of Zen. It is said that he spent nine years contemplating a wall in a lonely cave, but nevertheless managed to arouse enough public interest to be summoned before the emperor and to appoint a successor. When asked for an exposition of his philosophy, he replied in typically concise style:

A special transmission outside the scriptures;
No dependence on words or scriptures;
Direct pointing at the heart of man;
Seeing into one's own nature.

A typical Zen story relates to the Second Patriarch, *Hui-Ke*. In a desperate search for the realization that Bodhidharma was said to possess, he waited for days outside the cave. Eventually his patience gave out, and in his torment, he cut off his right arm. He then stormed into the Patriarch's presence and offered the severed limb as a token of his sincerity. The following conversation ensued:

Hui-Ke: Please pacify my mind.

Bodhidharma: Bring your mind before me.

Hui-Ke: I cannot produce my mind.

Bodhidharma: There – I have pacified your mind.

On receiving this reply, Hui-Ke attained *satori*: realization of the true nature of reality, a state of ultimate intuitive certainty.

There are many such stories about a disciple achieving realization after hearing a few words from a master. Zen, with its love of directness and simplicity, tells the story as economically as possible. What is significant is not the actual words of the master, but his choosing of the exact time, place and expression to best open the disciple's mind. The student's intellectual baggage must be reduced to the absolute minimum so as not to impede his vision of the greater reality. The history of Zen does not focus on vast convocations of clergy, the transmission of abstruse philosophy, or mass conversions, but rather on mundane events in the lives of masters and students. In Zen, the present situation is everything, perfect in its totality, and the task of the student is to appreciate that perfection. Opinions, wishes, dreams, ideals, and commentaries are not only otiose but are also distractions from the job at hand.

The growth of Zen Buddhism

The popularity of Zen grew rapidly in China over the next few centuries. The next great figure in Chinese Zen was the Sixth Patriarch, *Hui-Neng* (638–713 CE), an illiterate wood-cutter who is said to have become enlightened after hearing a recitation of the *Diamond Sutra*. As he did not appoint a successor, the line of Patriarchs ceased, but Zen continued to flourish over the next two centuries. Much of the material studied by Zen students in later centuries comes from incidents and conversations in the lives of the masters who flourished during this period. Many schools of Zen philosophy developed, but in the end, two major schools prevailed:

- *Lin Chi* (*Rinzai* in Japanese), or *Sudden School of Enlightenment*, named after its founding master;
- *Tsao Tung* (*Soto* in Japanese), or *Gradual School of Enlightenment*.

Other schools either joined forces with one of these two schools or faded into obscurity with the death of their chief master. Buddhism, and Zen, in particular, continued to be a powerful cultural force in China until the colonial era and the introduction of Christianity. After the Communists came into power in 1949, the hold of Buddhism was further weakened, although monasteries have continued to operate.

The *Lin-Chi* school was introduced into Japan by the monk *Eisai* in 1191 CE. Zen spread rapidly in Japan, which is today the Mecca for students of Zen. The Japanese, with their assiduous efforts to preserve all elements of their historical culture, are probably responsible for the survival of Zen and certainly for its transmission to the West. While some may argue that by formalizing the practice of Zen very rigorously, the Japanese have killed its spirit and have reduced it to just another form of religious observance, it cannot be denied that without their efforts, Zen would probably be a footnote rather than a major chapter in the history of religion.

Zen in practice

Zen is the most paradoxical form of religious expression. It aims for the highest level of spiritual realization but uses the most mundane of means. It appears that in the earliest period of Zen, these means were not fixed but evolved spontaneously in the master. As Zen was a direct transmission, mastery involved not merely demonstrating the highest level of awareness, but also drawing students up to the level of their master. The master, intuitively aware of the needs and aspirations of each disciple, would choose the most appropriate act, gesture, word, or article to promote the individual student's insight.

Zen is built on the view that the eternal verities associated with human existence cannot be expressed intellectually, and that understanding springs from awareness. Doctrinal expositions about ontological origins and final ends of life are eschewed, and the student is encouraged to probe actuality as presented by the events in his daily life. Life itself is viewed as a narrow strip extending between two gulfs of nothingness; it becomes beautiful and meaningful when one becomes fully aware of its briefness and un-repeatableness.

Here is a classic Zen parable: *A man is pursued by a ravenous tiger through a forest, and finds himself in a clearing at the edge of a two-hundred-foot cliff. Peering over the edge, he can see that the cliff terminates in a broad ledge below. Seeking to climb down, he sees a wild strawberry vine that extends down to the ledge. With great caution, he clasps the vine and starts to make a slow descent. On the way, he hears a roar from below, and looking down, he sees another tiger on the ledge. He also becomes aware that the vine is slowly becoming detached from the surface of the cliff, and that it will not be able to support his weight for much longer. He then notices that, at the limit of his reach, is a single fully grown wild strawberry. With great care, he manages to pluck the fruit and drop it into his mouth. He finds that it is the most delicious strawberry that he ever tasted: in fact, it seems that he had never previously really tasted a strawberry.*

Much of Zen history consists of catalogues of words and deeds of the masters and the reactions of their students. Zen eschews the popular human practices of discussion, persuasion, and intimidation: these are viewed as games played by people crowding their lives with intellectual furniture to block out the sight of the truth. After all, Zen is an essential part of the culture of Buddhism, which seeks to offer an escape from the everlasting wheel of birth and death. But unlike the schools of *Hinayana* Buddhism, which schools its devotees through precept, study, and observances, Zen impatiently discards anything which is only a representation of reality. The truth, the perennial key to all the mysteries of creation and beyond, lies in front of us: it does not require description or interpretation. All we need to do is realize the agonizing uniqueness of every moment, a totality of experience to which nothing can be added or taken away.

Daily life

Many people may say that they take life as it comes, but few really do. A master, when asked to describe his practice of Zen, replied: "When hungry I eat, and when tired I sleep." The questioner, bewildered with the simplicity of this reply, objected: "But that is what ordinary people do." The master disagreed: "No, they do not. For when they eat, their minds are on a thousand other things and when they sleep, they toss and turn, tortured by a thousand dreams."

This interchange reveals many important aspects of Zen. The first may be summarized thus:

There is nothing extraordinary apart from ordinary things.

Zen monks have sung that drawing water and chopping wood are indeed miraculous acts. Miraculous they are indeed, but not in the sense of the miracles sought by a sensation-loving public. Miracles today are considered primarily to be suspensions of the laws of nature – events that suggest the hand of an external omnipotent agency. To the genuine student of Zen, such idiosyncratic demonstrations are of little value: to him an actual event unfolding in the continuous flux of the phenomenal world is miraculous because of its uniqueness. The world of actual rather than interpreted happenings is fascinating because of the continuous dissolution of form. The Zen seeker wants to get behind the action to see the actual machinery of causation at work. What he seeks is absolute intuitive knowledge: in the final analysis, things can only be perceived, not proven.

The world

The second important aspect of Zen relates to the way that we express and justify our view of the world. When I was being guided through the intricacies of the Italian language, one of my lecturers made a most interesting point. When we were discussing the subjunctive mood, he observed that the use of this form indicated that the event discussed had never occurred.

We spend much of our lives worrying about such events. Mark Twain wryly observed that there had been a lot of bad things in his life, and that most of them had never happened. Fear and expectation colour our view of our lives so much so that we often deprive ourselves of valuable opportunities in the present, which is, after all, the only space of time in which we can operate. So much activity in the world is pure contingency, as is the massing of armed forces, the availability of public education, and the dynamics of religious subscription. "Sufficient unto the day is the evil thereof" (Matthew 6:34) is a maxim esteemed in Zen even more than in Christianity. Why discuss what has not happened when so much is happening before our eyes?

The koan

The third important aspect of Zen, which again underscores its paradoxical nature, is the development of techniques that promote a state of realization. The one that is most famous, although not always most significant, is the *koan*. This term comes from Chinese *kung'an*, the literal meaning of which is "transcript of an official document." The corruption of this expression is in itself typical of the wry humour of Zen. A *koan*, developed fully as a practice by the fierce master *Lin Chi* (*Rinzai* in Japanese, *d*. 967 CE), is a true conundrum; it is a statement, question, or reply to a question that is on the surface illogical, impossible or nonsensical.

Possibly the most famous *koan* is that of the Japanese master *Hakuin* (1685–1768):

What is the sound of the clapping of one hand?

There is no solution in the conventional sense to such a question. In investigating this conundrum, the student must cast away all his mental props, leaving an untainted mind to pierce into the heart of the question. The intermediate result of this investigation is a "doubt sensation", an intense psychophysical state in which all habitual modes of thought are shaken loose from their foundations. For those that persist, a new state of clarity arises in which the problem posed by the *koan* is seen for what it is: a problem created by the limitations of the mind. When this realization comes, duality is robbed of its grip: *soluble and insoluble* become just another pair of inevitable opposites, like good and bad, pleasure and pain, life and death. The sound of the clapping of one hand is then allowed to resound in its own space without hindrance by the Zen aspirant as he continues on his trackless path.

There are other koans that are on the surface rational questions, but which require a Zen rather than logical response. The most famous of these is:

What is the meaning of Bodhidharma's coming from the West?

The most famous reply is that of *Chao Chou* (778–897 CE):

The cypress tree in the courtyard.

Seeking to place an irrational response in a rational framework, the novice wonders why the master replied in this fashion. After the student has "worked through" the *koan*, he will understand that the master's reply was a spontaneous actuality. A question was asked; he replied. Nothing more and nothing less. To hang a commentary or interpretation of this event would be, in the words of a Cha'an master "like adding another head to one already on your shoulders."

With vast public education systems and banks of knowledge in the West today, the *koan* has lost much of its original power, becoming a quaint artistic artefact that fits neatly into a category labeled "Zen." Furthermore, the purpose for which *koans* were developed i.e. to challenge all preconceptions of a student and force him into an area where the intellect could no longer operate, is now considered improper, if not dangerous. Trauma is something we try to palliate or avoid in this analgesic age. Few people see any reason to disturb the powerful luxury of middle-class existence. Why meditate in the cold when you can watch television in air-conditioned comfort?

However, the *koan* is an example of what Zen appears to abhor: a contingency device. It was designed to create the most massive psychological crisis that a student could sustain, but under the guidance of a master who knew precisely the limits of the student's endurance. When the student finally succeeded in attaining realization, he knew that nothing could ever again threaten his peace of mind. Whatever happened, he would be able to accept and deal with it efficiently, with no fear, regret, or hesitation.

In the broadest sense, the concept of the *koan* is still with us. When threatened with disaster, sudden ill-health, or deep grief, we are unwillingly subjected to the experience deliberately sought by the Zen student. The following dialogue between *Chao Chou* (778–897), one of the greatest Chinese *Cha'an* masters, and a student encapsulates the Zen approach to such problems:

Student: What should I do if I am carrying nothing with me?
Chao Chou: Lay it down.

Student: And if I cannot lay it down?

Chao Chou: Then carry it with you.

This interchange expresses in the most direct terms the experience of grief. Those who have unexpectedly lost a loved one often feel the grief as an almost physical burden, which they are able neither to keep carrying nor to put down. It appears that no one can avoid sharp and bitter clashes with unenviable circumstances – and the most momentous of these become our own *koans*.

Grief

The process of grieving has been studied in depth and two principles have been consistently validated:

- Grieving is a natural process that involves the whole person: body, mind and spirit;
- Grieving works its own course: the process cannot be shortened or alleviated by argument, medication or diversion.

An obvious case where grieving will occur naturally is the passing of a loved one. The resolution of grieving will come when one accepts the unhappy circumstance as a natural, proper and inevitable event. Similarly, the Zen student comes to realize that all is in the mind, and the mind, whose identity and faculties he once thought to be so much under threat, is a toy – a device constituted of the ephemera that it wishes to interpret. What is real is the *No-Mind*: an entity not conditioned by anything, the invisible blackboard on which the history of the universe is written. As the chalk is rubbed off the blackboard remains, affected neither by what has been inscribed on it nor by the possibility that it may remain blank indefinitely. It should be noted that, since it cannot be restricted by definition, the *No-Mind* is neither existent nor non-existent: it is completely beyond qualification. It is the "is-ness" that remains when the duality of existence/non-existence is left behind.

The final stage in the grieving process is release, not palliation of anguish. In my view true resolution of such grief requires satisfaction of three expectations:

- That the passing of the loved one was an appropriate event, i.e. that it has a justifiable place in one's emotional history;
- That the loved one is in a happy state of mind i.e. that he/she is able to accept his death;
- That the space in the mourner's life created by the departure of the loved one has been filled, either by another person or a change in circumstances.

It should be noted that all of these happen in the mind of the mourner, who is the only person who can decide when he is ready to get on with life. None of these could be called events because they represent changes in perception rather than the machinations of outside forces.

Zen and the mind

The Zen student eventually realizes that everything, i.e. "every*thing*," is in the mind, which operates by defining and separating entities comparatively. To eat an orange, to read a book, or to die are merely activities; it is we who decide whether they are pleasant or unpleasant, desirable or undesirable, easy or difficult, joyful or tragic.

Zen has sometimes been called *mind murder*, and in a sense it is. But it is a murder without a body: "Nobody's funeral, for there is no one to bury", as T. S. Eliot puts it in *East Coker*. Many people fear that once the mental furniture has been removed, one will become dull and joyless, shuffling through life like a pallid automaton. However, nothing could be further from the truth. Zen is about the joy of activity, with fearless and spontaneous participation in all aspects of life. What remains – after the obsession with the duality of joy and sorrow has been put aside – is a positive state of equanimity, a world in which one laughs and cries, but ceases to be troubled by the memory of laughter and tears. The Zen student sees trauma, not as an inescapable process of cause and effect, but as unnecessary mental baggage. To paraphrase *Chao Chou*, if one is carrying something, one can put it down.

This image illustrates that Zen can and does make intelligent use of dualistic principles. The machinery of the dualistic universe is there for us to use: how well we use it is up to us. Any grievance we may nurture about the way in which the world operates is merely another load we impose on ourselves; any complaint is merely a request for someone else to do a job that we should be doing ourselves. Zen also points out that when we think dualistically, we often create situations that we don't want. Those with an obsessive fear of disease, death, or other undesirable things often draw those events towards them. What is needed to deal effectively with problems of life is a fearless and buoyant spirit, and a clear and incisive mind. While the practice of Zen in its formal regime may be impractical for many people, everyone can benefit from applying its principles in daily life.

Zen for everyday living

Is there, then, a general Zen principle that one can apply to everyday living? There is, and it can be expressed thus:

> *Always act without ulterior motive*

The actions of daily life are complete experiences in themselves, and require our full attention. Another anecdote involving Chao Chou illustrates the application of this intensity:

A young monk had just finished his breakfast, and hurried up to the master, eager to start his study of Zen.

The master asked: "Have you finished your breakfast?"

The student replied that he had.

"Then wash your bowl," ordered the master, and the young monk's eyes were opened. He realized with a sudden certainty the immediacy of experience and that nothing existed apart from the here and now.

When we plan or perform an action to achieve an end that is not immediately related to the action, we are trying to take reality and crush it into an arbitrary set of circumstances. Zen masters point out that all the delusive emotions of expectancy, joy, disappointment, anger and envy all flow from the false interpretations we place upon events.

Two men, both in good health and athletically gifted, may be swimming side by side in a river. One man has just become prosperous after years of struggle, and his swimming reflects his joyous mood. The other has recently been forced into bankruptcy and his wife has left him; he drags his way through the water feeling that he could drown in misery. Yet in the here and now, the relevant circumstances of the men are identical: both are able, healthy and involved in the same recreational activity at the same time. The joy of one and the misery of the other are pieces of irrelevant mental baggage that they have chosen by habit to carry with them.

Zen does not suggest that we should live aimlessly, without planning or morality. The Zen approach to planning is to plan, and then let the plan work itself out. In reality, man cannot create anything: all he can do is to arrange the furniture in his environment to enable certain active entities to come together so that a new entity or experience can be generated. With regard to morality, Zen would say that observance of social mores is important, but that this should be done for its own sake, not for any expected advantage.

What the practice of Zen strives to do is to liberate the aspirant from fear and attachment. Once freed from these impediments, a person can act spontaneously and productively, secure in the knowledge that he is part of the inexhaustible, if illusory, panoply of the phenomenal world.

As the Buddhists say, we can never escape the toils of *samsara* (the world of duality), until we realize that it and the *Void* are one and the same thing. With this realization comes the powerful sense of release that allows one to act efficiently and joyfully, without expectation of reward or fear of retribution. What Zen adds to this uplifting experience is humour and an appreciation of the exquisite irony of duality. As one Japanese master observed:

The winter is so cold and the cherry blossoms of spring are so beautiful,

and one would be incomplete without the other.

The Heart Sutra

The vast canon of *Mahayana Buddhism* includes a number of *sutras* or *explanatory expositions of doctrine*. Many of these are in the form of dialogue, similar in structure to the Socratic dialogues of Plato.

A group of *sutras* from the first century CE were gathered in a collection called the *Perfection of Wisdom Sutras*. One of the most celebrated of these is the *Prajna Paramita Heart Sutra*, which is still recited daily in Buddhist monasteries across the world. It is considered possibly the most intense and advanced statement of Buddhist philosophy.

One of the most striking features of this *sutra* is its brevity – it is only about 300 words in English translation. Another major feature is its boldness. It commences with the deliberations of the Buddha, *Avalokitesvara*, on the insubstantiality of the world of manifestation. He then proceeds to examine the fundamental doctrines of Buddhism and finds them equally insubstantial. The *Five Skandhas* are found to be unreal, as is the *Noble Eightfold Path*. Having totally freed himself from the practices of categorization and calculation, the Buddha realizes supreme wisdom and merges into the state of total 'beyondness.'

A focused reading of this sutra, even in translation, can induce the feeling of total cleansing of the mind. As one progresses through the series of gentle negations, it is as though opaque films are being removed from the inner apprehension, allowing the perception of a scarcely visible luminous core. For a brief time, the preoccupations of daily life seem trivial, mere mental noise of which one is faintly aware, minuscule in comparison to the thunderous silence of the *Void*.

The *sutra* commences with the denial of the substance of form. The constituents of form having been established as void, the Buddha then realizes that actions associated with form are equally insubstantial. There is no path, and no one to traverse the path.

Origin of the Heart Sutra

As with much scripture, the identity of the author is unknown. However, the ideas which the *sutra* develops can be traced to one of the most famous incidents in the history of Zen Buddhism. The Fifth Chinese Patriarch, *Hung-Jan* (601–674 CE), felt that he was coming to the end of his life and wished to nominate a successor. Accordingly, he invited monks to submit a stanza that would illustrate their understanding of Zen. The chief monk and heir apparent, *Shen Hsui*, composed the following verse and wrote it on a wall:

The body is the Bodhi-tree;
The mind is like a mirror bright.
Take heed to keep it always clean,
And let no dust alight.

A semi-literate kitchen hand, Hui Neng (638–713 CE), saw this poem and decided that he could do better. Accordingly, he arranged for a fellow monk to inscribe the following verse on the wall next to that of Shen Hsui:

There is no Bodhi-tree,
No stand of mirror bright.
Since all is void
Where can the dust alight?

The Fifth Patriarch realized that Hui Neng had the true understanding of Zen, and summoned the ill-educated monk for a secret conference. Hui Neng was invested with the insignia of patriarchal office – and then advised to flee for his life to escape the expected retribution from jealous supporters of Shen Hsui! Later Hui Neng was publicly accepted as the Sixth Patriarch, and is today recognized as one of the seminal figures in the history of Zen.

In Japanese Zen, this state of ultimate enlightenment is called "Jijimuge" which D. T. Suzuki translates as "the unimpeded interdiffusion of all particulars."

The Heart Sutra

My translation given below has been adapted from a number of sources. While no guarantee is given of its accuracy, I feel that it captures the spirit of the original to the best of my understanding.

When the Divine Lord of Compassion
Was absorbed in the observation of Perfect Wisdom,
He perceived that all Five Skandhas were empty.
Thus He overcame all ills and suffering.

Oh, seeker after truth, know that
Form does not differ from the Void, and the Void does not differ from Form.
Form is Void and Void is Form;
The same is true for Sensations, Perceptions, Volitions and Consciousness.

Oh seeker, the Characteristics of the Voidness of All Things
Are Non-Arising and Non-Ceasing,
Non-Defiled and Non-Pure,
Non-Increasing and Non-Decreasing.

Therefore, in the Void, there are no Forms, no Sensations, no Perceptions, no Volitions, and no Consciousness.

There is no Eye, Ear, Nose, Tongue, Body, or Mind;
No Form, Sound, Smell, Taste, Touch, or Object in the Mind;
Nothing to be seen and no field of Consciousness.

There is no Ignorance
And also no Ending of Ignorance:
There is no Old Age and Death
And also no Ending of Old Age and Death.

There is no Truth of Suffering,
There is no Cause of Suffering,
There is no Cessation of Suffering,
And no path to freedom from Suffering.

There is no Wisdom,
And there is no attainment whatsoever.

Because there is nothing to be attained,
The Bodhisattva, relying on perfect wisdom, has no obstruction in his mind.

Because there is no obstruction, he has no fear,
And he passes far beyond confused imagination,
And reaches ultimate bliss.

The Buddhas of the Past, Present and Future,
By relying on Perfect Wisdom,
Have attained Supreme Enlightenment.

Therefore, the Perfect Wisdom is the mighty Invocation,
The Invocation of Illumination,
The Supreme Invocation, which can truly protect one from all suffering forever.

Hear the words of the exemplar of Perfect Wisdom as he proclaims:

All is gone,
gone,
gone now,
gone forever.
Awakened!
So be it!

The Art of Non-Expert Living – Oberon Michaels

Chapter 3: The Path

How hard should life be?

"Life isn't meant to be easy"

– Ayn Rand

Like many famous sayings considered to enshrine some deep wisdom, Ayn Rand's raises more questions than it answers. Firstly, the use of the word 'meant' suggests belief in a presiding deity or system that decides how the individual experiences life. The word 'easy' further complicates the matter: easy for whom? The deity or the individual?

Ease refers to a lack of constriction and forced effort. That which is truly *easy* one just does, often without premeditation, like a cat scaling a wall. Given that so many processes in human existence, and particularly in the human body, are automated, it would seem that an existence in which the majority of activities required concentrated and arduous effort would not be sustainable. Genuine difficulty occurs when a person is unable to perform actions that come naturally for the majority of people: for example, the person crippled with arthritis may have a very limited range of movement. Or someone who is afflicted with severe allergies may find themselves barred from many activities or locations. For the rest of us, we stroll along the street, greet our neighbours and eat our dinner with little consciousness that we are doing things that other organisms might consider miracles of skill and organization.

To suggest that life is a continual process of frustration, lightened only by the gleam of a distant reward is, to me, neither helpful nor encouraging. Underlying the belief that life is not easy is a conditioned pursuit of reward.

But what are we striving for? The religious devotee longs for heaven after death: a state in which all is enjoyment and effort is absent. The more materialistic among us strive to build a personal environment of such abundance that any sense of want or possible shortage is extirpated. The warrior wants an endless campaign of crushing victories, in which he can revel in his sense of power and enjoy the righteousness of eliminating the agents of evil.

Needless to say, in this life, we never seem to get there. Enough is never enough – human beings do not do satisfaction well. Some say we suffer because of our inherent unworthiness, our human limitedness. However, I would rather suggest that our pain is due to our dependence on rewards, which are essentially ephemeral.

The *Bhagavad Gita* recommends that we should not seek the fruits of action. Jesus said to take no thought for the morrow. He also said (Matt. 11:30):

> "For my yoke *is* easy, and my burden is light."

Many religions seek to address the obvious inequalities of life by proposing that there is a future permanent state of existence in which all of these will be addressed and rectified. This proposition seems to be based on a quirky distortion of logic:

1. Man is an imperfect being living in an imperfect world.
2. Man has an intrinsic desire to reach and experience perfection.
3. This desire originates in an intuition that such a state of perfection exists.
4. As perfection is unattainable in this world, it must be available in another.
5. If this perfect world exists it must also be enteral and unchanging.

Hence, in many cases, the concept of an afterlife has been developed, in which the irreducible core of man, stripped of temporal limitations, will continue to exist forever. However, Buddhism denies the concept of an enduring self, or "soul" as it would be considered in Christianity, and focuses on the management of life in the present. Oddly enough, this accords with one of the most famous sayings of Jesus (Matt. 6:34):

"Take therefore no thought for the morrow: for the morrow shall take thought for the things of itself. Sufficient unto the day is the evil thereof."

None of the above is intended to deny or dishonour the undoubted and terrible suffering that abounds in this world—the devastation and dislocation wrought by war, the agonies induced by severe disease, or the grinding poverty unjustly endured by so many. However, for those of us who have the good fortune to enjoy lives of relative comfort and prosperity, perhaps we should be finding joy in our immediate surroundings rather than hankering after an experience of perfection which can never be ours. But we can have a lot of ease – if we allow ourselves.   And one of the effective ways to do this is to apply the general principles of Buddhism. We may perceive a particular set of circumstances to be pleasant or unpleasant, easy or difficult: but regardless of our personal assessment, the cosmos continues to operate in its own way. Therefore, the wisest course would appear to be to put ourselves in sync with the current of the universe, rather than trying to change it.

Truth

How do we know something is true?   Because we are persuaded it is true.

Even hardened religious apologists will agree that listeners are rarely converted solely by argument.   While the logic and rhetorical force of apologetic presentation may be powerful, even enthralling, it does not often lead to agreement.

The acceptance of an opinion or a philosophical or religious proposition appears to be related to an inner sympathetic resonance which is experienced as a visceral response. Those who experience religious conversion often speak of a feeling of compelling, even overwhelming, conviction. The source of this is frequently attributed to the intervention of an intangible spiritual entity, which could be a discarnate prophet, or even the voice of God himself. Hence, truth is often regarded as requiring a creator and an agency of transmission. By extension, the purveyor of this truth often comes to be regarded as inerrant and omniscient.

While conservative apologists decry the modern respect paid to personal feelings, religious conviction is essentially based on emotion. The religious devotee speaks of experiencing the "truth of the Gospel" in his heart. He feels his love for Jesus, an absent personality whom he clothes with the qualities that he expects a savior to have, becoming deep and revivifying the devotee's whole person. This is, in essence, a visceral response generated by feelings, and consciously amplified by devotion.

Examples of emotive devotion are abundant in Roman Catholicism, with its heavy emphasis on paying homage to the aristocracy of sanctity, notably the Virgin Mary, Joseph, and the prominent figures of the apostolic age. According to the detailed hagiography of the Virgin which is promoted by conservative Catholic peak groups like the Fatima Centre (https://fatima.org), Mary is the archetypal mother of all created beings, due to whose persuasive restraint, God has been prevented – so far – from destroying a world which is radically infested with sin. The devotion of subscribers to the Marian cult is patently emotional, as is the range of feelings and impulses attributed to the Virgin herself, both during her life on earth, and posthumously, as she goes about her work of saving the world.

The sympathetic resonance that evokes the adoption of a particular viewpoint also applies outside of the strictly religious realm. Anyone who develops a passion for any activity is inspired by this feeling. For example, the musician feels that music 'speaks' to him, inducing a spontaneous concordance and leading him to an enhanced ability to understand and reproduce a piece in performance. The same applies to every other discipline or activity.

Hence the question arises: what drives this concordance of resonance? Is it the effort of the person or the attraction of the environment?

Inspirational environments

The Bible, which many people find inspiring, has left me cold. By contrast, I find Zen parables to be moving and instructive, and exposure to the basic doctrines of Buddhism reassuring and inspiring. The most "religious" experience I have had has come from reading the Heart Sutra. I find that reading or hearing its gentle catalogue of negations induces a delightful state of calm, a lifting of the veil of worry that surrounds much of our thinking.

Religious devotees are encouraged to believe that holy places or revered liturgies possess intrinsic power to change and elevate the fundamental personality. Roman Catholic doctrine, drawing on the Aristotelian assumptions of Thomas Aquinas, proposes that everything has an essence (its basic "thingness") and an "accidental" presentation i.e. an appearance or phenomenal representation. Hence, the supposed "miracle" of transubstantiation – in which the essence of the communion wafer is converted into the actual body of Christ, while it remains unchanged in appearance and physical qualities. Similarly, the sacred space of a cathedral is understood as invested with the spirit of the Divine.

I think that for each person, certain environments awaken positive neural responses. I too find the peaceful atmosphere of a church emotionally relaxing and nourishing. However, I believe that this impression is stimulated by the careful crafting of the environment, the restrained and quiet behavior of worshippers, the measured pace of all proceedings, and the avoidance of conversational challenge. In fact, all extensive spaces where there is an absence of human noise have the potential to induce this state of meditative awe.

What is Truth?

Christian religious apologists frequently inveigh against "personal truth" in contrast to God's "absolute truth", claiming that the former is entirely subjective – which is highly problematic when humanity is considered 'fallen', thoroughly corrupted by sin. Such apologists tend to warn of the chaos that would ensue should human beings be allowed to believe or affirm whatever *they* choose to see as true. What should be sought, these preachers say, is "objective" or "absolute truth" – those eternal monuments of verity which are proclaimed in scripture. However, religious and philosophical claims are not like rocks, whose appearance and basic constitution most people will unhesitatingly agree on. Truth claims require transmission, reception, translation and interpretation – all of which are subjective processes.

Our acceptance and deployment of truth appear to relate to our constitutional make-up, as delineated by the *Five Skandhas (Form, Sensation, Perception, Tendency, Consciousness)*. We are naturally attracted to principles that make our lives easier to navigate. The views that appeal to us, and which we defend, are those which appear to cement our place in the order of creation, and we use our talents and proclivities to justify those views. The religious apologist believes it to be true that to improve and indeed "save" the world, it is necessary that everyone should subscribe to his creed. The non-believer holds that in truth, there is no such thing as salvation, and hence no one to save and nothing to be saved from.

Hence, for you, truth is 'your truth.' If you should change your mind about any issue, including religion, the newly accepted truth is still 'your truth.' A person who goes through a series of religious conversions will assert, after each admission to a new religion, that he has now found the ultimate truth. For example, person X is born into a Muslim Family, becomes a convert to Calvinism at age twenty-five, and at age forty-five is admitted to the Roman Catholic Church. Had he died at age twenty, he could have felt secure that he would find himself in the Muslim paradise; had he died at age forty, he could have felt assured that he would be joining the tiny band of the elect in a Calvinist heaven; if he dies at the age of fifty, after receiving the last rites of the Roman Church, he could feel confident that he would be admitted to permanent felicity among fellow Catholics. At any of these points, he could claim that he was in possession of the truth necessary for salvation.

Freedom

Then you will know the truth, and the truth will set you free.

Gospel of John 8:32

While the intention of this grandiose statement may be to provide a sense of certainty to Jesus' auditors, it raises more issues than it resolves. How is this freedom to be defined? Is it:

- Political freedom, i.e. from oppression?
- Physical freedom, i.e. from disease or the limitations of the body?
- Intellectual freedom, i.e. freedom to explore belief systems and subscribe to those of one's choosing?
- Environmental freedom, i.e. from the tyranny of hostile forces of nature?
- Financial freedom, i.e. to accumulate sufficient personal resources to enjoy a happy and productive life?
- Existential freedom, i.e. from the questions of life that seem to have no answers or cause pain and suffering?

While these are generally agreed to be worthwhile and desirable outcomes, this verse is most likely referring to theological freedom: freedom from the burden of sin and freedom from the wrath of God.

While the above-named forms of freedom (political, physical, intellectual, environmental and financial) are to a significant degree interlinked, they have little in common with theological freedom.

An alternative understanding of freedom

A more helpful scriptural invocation comes from the *Bhavagad Gita,* the scriptural tale that forms part of the great Hindu classic, the Mahabharata. In chapter three, Krishna instructs the irresolute Arjuna:

> *Man does not enjoy freedom from action, from the non-commencement of that which he has to do; nor does he obtain happiness from total inactivity. Every man is involuntarily urged to act by those principles which are inherent in his nature. So the man is praised, who having subdued all his passions, performs with his active faculties all the functions of life, unconcerned about the event. Perform the settled action: action is preferable to inaction.*
>
> (Adapted from the translation by Charles Wilkins)

Lester Levenson, the creator of the *Sedona Method*, a self-help protocol built around a process of structured questioning, spoke of ultimate personal success as "going free." This is a state in which the emotions and drives which skew our view of reality are seen for what they are: screens that colour or obscure our vision of the immaculate consciousness that is our true nature. Levenson also describes this consciousness as "is-ness" or "am-ness," the unified vision that arises from the merging of the object, the viewer of the object, and the act of viewing – the experience of non-duality.

In a world of contingency, there are some processes to which we are unavoidably subject. To remain alive, we must breathe, we must eat, and we must operate in harmony with the furniture of our world. However, if we become aware of the forces which are trying to drive us or constrain us, we can make more productive choices, and thus significantly expand our freedom of action.

Truly desirable freedom

Truly desirable freedom is freedom of positive action – the freedom to act in a way that will effectively address current problems and enable us to build a joyful and rewarding future.

The highest state of freedom is one in which negative conditions cannot affect a person – the freedom which has been described as *spiritual*.

Faith

It is ridiculous to speculate on what will exist when we cannot know.

– Plato (Lysis)

Faith: Pretending to know things you don't know.

– Dr Peter Boghossian, YouTube talk, May 21, 2012

Now, we shall have a complete definition of faith, if we say, that it is a steady and certain knowledge of the Divine benevolence towards us, which, being founded on the truth of the gratuitous promise in Christ, is both revealed to our minds, and confirmed to our hearts, by the Holy Spirit.

– John Calvin, Institutes of the Christian Religion, Book3, Chapter 2

Faith is a response to the revealing God.

– Bishop Robert Barron, in a YouTube conversation with Alex O'Connor, 2 April 2021

One of the best-known biblical definitions of religious faith is found in Hebrews 11:1–3:

"Now faith is the substance of things hoped for, the evidence of things not seen. For by it the elders obtained a good report. Through faith we understand that the worlds were framed by

> the word of God, so that things that are seen were not made of things that do appear."

Deities are by nature remote and mysterious – it is difficult to imagine that the man who collects the garbage is a Divine being, crowned with glory and possessing great power. Hence, the habitual hiddenness of deities has led to the codification of their messages in scripture. As they are deemed to be of divine origin, canonical scriptures are often held to be accurate, comprehensive, and without error, and this may lead to a situation where critical analysis is vigorously discouraged. The truth of books like the Bible and the Koran is often considered to be self-evident – the scripture is itself the proof of the claims it makes. In the hands of believers, the findings of scientific research are often reinterpreted so that they can be used as evidence for the truth of scripture – and the more awkward conclusions reached by scientists are dismissed as either incorrect or unproven theory. On the other hand, the 'truths' propounded by religion are considered the products of Divine revelation – a source of knowledge held to be as valid (if not more so) as the process of reasoning from observation and experimentation.

One of the major problems in discussions about religion is the failure, or refusal, to distinguish between proof and evidence. Proof, or absolute verification of an action or a principle, is only possible in an intellectual environment, in which all parameters are defined and accepted, such as in mathematics or philosophy. In such disciplines, all irrelevant factors can be eliminated, and the resulting conclusion comes from examining the remaining pieces of the puzzle, as in the stark logic of a chess match. However, science does not seek for proofs but rather bodies of evidence that will support a theory. The proposition which has the greatest amount of confirmatory evidence and the least amount of conflicting evidence will be favoured. Of course, such propositions are subject to constant critical analysis, and hence to revision or even abandonment when justified.

A useful comparison can be made with the game of chess. It would be physically possible to open a chess board, place the pieces in any arrangement one chose, or even to add further pieces, and to move those pieces in any direction. However, everyone would agree that such an activity could not be defined as chess, unless the strict rules of the game were followed. Conventional theology can be viewed as following the same protocol: once one accepts a mass of underlying presuppositions, it can be seen as severely logical. However, once one presupposition is seriously challenged the whole structure is threatened with collapse. Of course, chess is just a game, not a set of prescriptions for ordering one's views and activities: one could agree with an opponent to change the rules of the game, without any consequences flowing into one's daily life. On the other hand, theology, with its prescribed beliefs and rituals, deliberately seeks to change and regulate the believer's existential framework.

The orbiting teapot

The impossibility of unchallengeable proofs in the natural world is illustrated in the celebrated example of Russell's teapot. Bertrand Russell, a lifelong atheist, proposed the possibility of a teapot orbiting the sun between Earth and

Mars. Because of its minuscule size, the teapot would not be observable by instruments on Earth, and the chances of a passing spacecraft encountering it would be vanishingly small. Furthermore, as its gravitational pull would be exiguous, it could have no measurable effect on conditions on Earth or Mars. Therefore, while it would be impossible to completely rule out the existence of such a teapot, for practical purposes its non-existence could be assumed.

However, if one chose, it would be possible to accept that the teapot existed, and that its disposition could have powerful effects on the earth. Arguing from effect to possible cause, a devotee of the Teapot cult could claim that powerful blessings flowed from the spout of the teapot, and any region at which the spout was pointed would flourish, and peace and harmony would abound there. Conversely, any area at which the handle of the teapot was inclined would experience disaster and destruction. Expanding the argument, the devotee could claim that the presiding deity of the teapot was arranging its movements to favour the upright and to punish the wicked. An example of this twisted logic is the assertion by the Roman Catholic Marian cult that World War II was caused by the failure of the world to heed the warnings given by the Virgin Mary in her visitations to the children at Fatima in Portugal in 1917. Cult followers conveniently ignore the fact that this unhappy prophecy did not become public knowledge until the fourth memoir of Fatima seer, Lucia Dos Santos was published in 1941 – two years after the start of the Second World War.

Clearly, it is reasonable to have faith in the existence of objects which are not apparent to the senses. Most people accept the existence of atoms and of bacteria, even though the shape and motion of such objects can only be detected with the help of advanced scientific equipment. However, research has consistently supported both atomic theory and germ theory, and much of our technology is built on the results of such research.

On the other hand, religious faith is dependent on accepting propositions that are admittedly not susceptible to regular experimental proof. Religious conversions are often attributed to an 'inner assurance', a personal conviction of Divine immanence, or the witnessing of a miracle. In other words, the feeling is that positive visceral resonance that underlies all deeply held convictions, whether religious or not. The person experiences an inner sense of validation, and then assumes that the stimulus provided by such validation represents a deep and powerful source of truth. Hence, the conversion experience of the born-again Christian and the deconversion experience of the former Christian are analogous: in both cases, the person's world has become more comprehensible and life is seen to be more manageable

The nature of belief

It is inaccurate to speak of a 'loss of faith.' We are all believing creatures, but we are also prone to changing and reviewing our beliefs – and indeed, this is a sign of healthy maturation and growth. The atheist does not 'believe less' than the religious devotee; rather, he believes different things. One may believe that a shrine is inhabited by a presiding deity, while another may hold that such a deity does not exist; both are beliefs.

A significant quality of a belief is that once it is lost, it is very difficult to recapture it. Professional magicians perform feats that appear to be impossible; once the trick is explained, it ceases to be magical. Magicians are keenly aware of this fact, and indeed, the celebrated practitioner Pen Jillette has stated that audiences should bear in mind that all his effects are achieved by trickery, and that magic should never be used to change anyone's basic beliefs. However, ritualistic religions like Roman Catholicism draw much of their power from the assertion of miraculous events that cause radical changes but which are untestable by ordinary means of investigation. Notable examples are the forgiveness of sins and transubstantiation. A person who loses belief in the actuality and efficacy of such events is unlikely to recover his faith in these processes.

Revelation

'Revelation' is a loaded term, which can be presented as having three meanings:

- Disclosure of a previously unknown, and often surprising fact;
- Realization of the nature of the beauty or significance of an event or artistic artefact;
- A message received directly from a deity

The word comes from a Latin root, which signifies the removal of a veil, or the removal of an obstacle clouding the perception or understanding of an artefact.

In all cases, the result is access to new knowledge for the recipient. The reception of the knowledge can have a profound effect on the individual.

Much of the doctrine of the Judeo-Christian religions is derived from a mysterious process of revelation, or disclosure of the Divine will. The source of such disclosures can be:

- Personal e.g. the inspired utterances of a saint or a prophet;
- Circumstantial e.g. Natural disasters or cataclysmic events, apparently designed to extirpate evil or terminate some undesirable social trend;
- Inductive e.g. The evidence of cosmic design

The thirteenth-century Catholic theologian, Thomas Aquinas, divided divine revelation into two categories:

- *Natural Revelation*, the demonstration of which is the power of the hidden God and his skill in establishing and maintaining order in a vast cosmos, and which should be apparent to all men;
- *Supernatural or Special Revelation*, in which arcane and life-defining truths are made available to the faithful through scripture or the deliberations of ecclesiastical officials.

The vitality of theology is dependent on the acceptance of revelation as unchallengeable and direct knowledge from an infallible source.

Complexity and controversy

Ironically, an organized religion appears to flourish in direct proportion to the complexity of its theology. An interesting example is Unitarian Universalism, which is one of the most reasonable and inclusive of all ecclesial groups. In a faith shorn of theological complexity, there is little for members to argue about, and hence minimal opportunity for contention. However, the membership of such ecclesial communities tends to remain small. By contrast, the largest church in world history, Roman Catholicism, which claims a nominal membership of about 17 percent of the world's population, has always been racked by controversy.

The first half-millennium of church history after Christ was dominated by heated debates over dogmatic issues, in particular the nature of Christ and the Trinity. The decision as to which opinions were correct, and hence canonical, was decided in the manner of political elections – by voting. Almost invariably, those who proposed doctrines that were simpler and more reasonable were defeated, and the most complex, baffling and irrational options were proclaimed as dogma. The most notorious example is probably the incomprehensible doctrine of the Trinity. The conclusions of theological speculation are converted into monuments of objective truth – and the epistemological engine which drives this process is divine revelation.

The 'smartest person in the room' strategy

A possible explanation of the cultivated complexity of Christian doctrine is that it represents an attempt to conceal the crassness of its basic premise: "Believe what we tell you, do what we say, or it will go badly with you." Religious apologists, especially Catholics, often work on the "smartest person in the room" strategy: this person is much smarter and better educated than you, so who are you to question what he says? In the days when illiteracy was widespread, and uneducated folk did not understand Latin (the language of ecclesiastical discourse) this gambit worked very well. Ironically, the Protestant revolution, one of the aims of which was to distribute scripture in the vernacular, produced a flurry of intellectual investigation which led to the Enlightenment and, later, the rejection of religious dogma.

The 'queen of the sciences'

Following the lead of Thomas Aquinas, the Catholic Church has proclaimed theology as the "Queen of the Sciences." In the *Summa Theologica* (First Part, Question One, Article Eight),

Aquinas makes the following claim, in justification of theology:

As other sciences do not argue in proof of their principles, but argue from their principles to demonstrate other truths in these sciences: so this doctrine does not argue in proof of its principles, which are the articles of faith, but from them, it goes on to prove something else.

In other words, the scientist is to blindly accept the validity of a proposition and then seek evidence to support it. Propositions which are considered to be the fruit of divine revelation are by definition unchallengeable and therefore should not be the subject of direct evaluation. Unsurprisingly, explanations by theologians are especially prone to confirmation bias.

Current scientific investigations are conducted on exactly opposite lines. Observations are made, data is collected and investigated, consistent patterns of structure and behaviour are noted, and operational principles are derived from the results. These principles are constantly subject to evaluation, and theories are changed or discarded when there is sufficient evidence of a new principle.

Belief and skepticism

In contrast to Christian definitions of revelation, the 'revelations' that abound in Hindu and Buddhist scripture generally have their origins in the intense cogitations of highly developed intellects. The calm deliberations of Hindu and Buddhist savants, often presented in the form of exhaustingly thorough dialogues with students, are refreshingly different from the puerile rantings of the Apostle Paul, whose message is often: "This saving message has been revealed to me, and it is the absolute truth, and if you don't believe it and do what I say, you will end up in Hell." In the Epistle to the Galatians 1:8–9, which is generally accepted by scholars as one of the genuine letters of Paul, the fiery apostle warns his congregants against paying heed to anyone who "preaches a different Gospel," and says that the faithful should not even continue to believe Paul himself, should he return with a changed message.

But though we, or an angel from heaven, preach any other gospel unto you than that which we have preached unto you, let him be accursed.

As we said before, so say I now again, If any man preach any other gospel unto you than that ye have received, let him be accursed.

It is interesting to note that the Letter to the Galatians is one of the earliest books in the New Testament, indicating that even in apostolic times doctrinal controversy was rampant.

Skepticism about Christ and his message has become widespread since the "search for the historical Jesus" movement commenced in the eighteenth century. Today, this trend has developed to the extreme of Christ Mythicism, in which a number of scholars have disputed the actual existence of Jesus. Unsurprisingly, defensive reaction from Christian theologians has been intense – if there is no Christ, the revelation attributed to him would likewise be non-existent. Even Paul was aware of the danger of disproof of the Christian revelation (I Corinthians 15:12–14):

Now if Christ be preached that he rose from the dead, how say some among you that there is no resurrection of the dead?

But if there be no resurrection of the dead, then is Christ not risen:

And if Christ be not risen, then is our preaching vain, and your faith is also vain.

Following this skeptical trend, the historical validity of other major figures like Buddha and Socrates has also been questioned. However, even if there were no historical Buddha or Socrates, the value of the teaching attributed to them would remain unchanged. The conclusions of their investigations can be readily subjected to testing in daily life, and can inform beliefs through behavioural experience – in contrast to approaches that seek to shape behaviour through enforced beliefs.

In Hinduism and Buddhism revelation flows from realization, not from instruction. The truth will make itself apparent to he who is ready to receive it.

Salvation

Organized religions share certain presuppositions:

- There is a spiritual dimension that lies beyond our present material world;
- That spiritual dimension is stable and eternal;
- There is a foundational link between the spiritual and material worlds;
- Human beings have the potential to move from one world to the other;
- To obtain permanent residence in the spiritual dimension, one must quit the material.

Religious controversy is often centered around the nature and accessibility of the spiritual dimension.

Salvation is the process by which the departed will be assured of an optimum existence in the afterlife.

Salvation vs enlightenment

Based on the above characteristics, it is nonsensical to describe theories like materialism or evolution as expressions of religion; they are philosophical worldviews that do not concern themselves with access to a spiritual dimension. Neither theory necessarily precludes a non-material reality, and there are in fact a large number of theistic evolutionists. Materialism denies the existence of a non-material dimension on the basis that that which exists must do so in time and space, and hence God's "existence" outside time and space is a logical impossibility.

In Christianity and Islam, the attainment of salvation is by the maintenance of particular beliefs and the performance of appropriate actions in a single life on this planet. Life is conceived as a moral obstacle course, at the end of which the soul is subject to judgement that will result in either elevation to Heaven or consignment to Hell for all eternity.

In Hinduism and Buddhism, the desired spiritual realization is liberation or enlightenment rather than salvation. After many cycles of life, the soul exhausts the load of *karma*, or consequences of action, and achieves a level of attainment which frees him from the formation of further desires which would have to be worked out in the phenomenal world. This is a state of supernal knowing, of psychological completeness, which no longer requires phenomenal expression.

Buddhist universalism

In its essence, Buddhism is universalist: it teaches that liberation is for all, and that it is, in fact, inevitable. Eventually, everyone will slough off all desire for identification with phenomena, and, as is said in Hindu scripture, "the dewdrop merges into the shining sea."

However, the "shining sea" is not a far distant realm: it is a non-contingent reality that is a permanent "now." Buddhist practice is devised to rejoice in the fullness of the present, in the realization that what is all that could be can be found in the moment. Memory is not annihilated, but is seen as images recalled from a vanished past.

For the Ancient Greeks, the paradise of *Elysium* could only be entered if the soul drank from two streams, first Lethe and then

Eunoe. After drinking from the first, all memories would be completely expunged; after drinking from the second, the memories would be restored but totally stripped of all associated trauma. This process can be equated with the admonition of Cha'an Master Chao Chou: "Carry nothing with you."

The celebrated Hindu mystic, *Ramana Maharshi*, expressed this thought as follows: "When you get on a train, you do not continue to carry your luggage with you: you allow the train to do the carrying." The Now is inherently sufficient: liberation is a state of total continuous awareness of the Now, which does not arouse regret or desire for change, but which will accommodate both.

Salvation is clearly a process of getting somewhere; liberation is the process of removing the need to get somewhere.

Some have argued that the Buddhist attitude is intrinsically fatalistic – that one should blandly acquiesce with the up and downs of mortal existence. Furthermore, some say that Buddhism is functionally amoral – what is the stimulus for people to be good if there were no promise of reward or threat of punishment? Neither of these views is sustainable. The Buddhist seeks to develop a compassion that embraces all beings in the cosmos and a dynamic introspection that lends fascination to the processes and phenomena of the universe.

The afterlife

It is interesting to compare the Judeo-Christian and Hindu/Buddhist views of our eternal destination. The New Testament doesn't say a lot about Heaven other than to stress that Jesus will be sitting at the right hand of the Father. (Matthew 26:64, 1 Peter 3:22). The *right-hand* motif is also expressed in Psalm 110: "The Lord says to my Lord: Sit at My right hand." Heaven is primarily a place where God rewards those who have been suitably obedient to his word. The geography of the Divine abode is not described, but it is said that there is an impassable gulf between Heaven and Hell.

In the Second Letter to Corinthians 12:1–5, Paul recounts the following vision:

It is not expedient for me doubtless to glory. I will come to visions and revelations of the Lord.

I knew a man in Christ above fourteen years ago, (whether in the body, I cannot tell; or whether out of the body, I cannot tell: God knoweth;) such a one caught up to the third heaven.

And I knew such a man, (whether in the body, or out of the body, I cannot tell: God knoweth;)

How that he was caught up into paradise, and heard unspeakable words, which it is not lawful for a man to utter.

Of such an one will I glory: yet of myself I will not glory, but in mine infirmities.

In other words, Heaven is an indescribably fantastic place and Paul won't say any more about it.

On the other hand, the Gospels are a little more forthcoming about the horrors of Hell.

Matthew 8:11–12:

And I say unto you, That many shall come from the east and west, and shall sit down with Abraham, and Isaac, and Jacob, in the kingdom of heaven.

But the children of the kingdom shall be cast out into outer darkness: there shall be weeping and gnashing of teeth.

Luke 13:28–30:

There shall be weeping and gnashing of teeth, when ye shall see Abraham, and Isaac, and Jacob, and all the prophets, in the kingdom of God, and you yourselves thrust out.

And they shall come from the east, and from the west, and from the north, and from the south, and shall sit down in the kingdom of God.

And, behold, there are last which shall be first, and there are first which shall be last.

Revelation 20:13–15:

And the sea gave up the dead which were in it; and death and hell delivered up the dead which were in them: and they were judged every man according to their works.

And death and hell were cast into the lake of fire. This is the second death.

And whosoever was not found written in the book of life was cast into the lake of fire.

The most detailed description of the infernal region can be found in the apocryphal book, *Apocalypse of Peter*, in which specific punishments are allocated for particular sins. Fire and bodily piercing feature prominently among the retributive treatments. A similar arrangement of the underworld is employed in the classic text, *Dante's Inferno*.

Catholic dogma proposes an additional afterlife region: Purgatory, in which souls who are destined for Heaven, but who are not immediately fit for entry due to the lingering effects of sin, are cleansed, or made perfect in the sight of God. Such souls will not be damned, but may be required to suffer pains similar to those inflicted in Hell in the course of purification. The Catholic Encyclopedia of 1913 defines Purgatory as 'a place or condition of punishment, who, departing this life in God's grace, are not entirely free from venial faults or have not fully paid the satisfaction due to their transgression.' The article goes on to state that this doctrine is "clearly the teaching of scripture" and has been ratified by a number of church councils. Many Protestant sects reject the doctrine as being "unbiblical" and heretical, and hold that those holding it are facing eternal damnation.

Hinduism and Buddhism also propose extensive afterlife geographies but these are held to be temporary states. Until it reaches liberation, the soul shuttles between non-physical regions and human life in repeated incarnations, as required by the law of *karma*. Therefore, the final aim of religious practice is not admission to a particular post-life paradise, but is to achieve the level of realization which carries one to the ultimate undifferentiated state, which is defined in a trinitarian form in Hinduism as *Existence-Knowledge-Bliss*.

Path or circle?

The process of salvation is a path; it starts at human birth and concludes at the point of divine judgement. In the West, organized religions have a central purpose – to enable their subscribers to achieve a pass mark in the posthumous moral examination, and thus gain admittance to heaven. While it is true that it is commanded that believers practise "Christian charity" (Matthew 25:31–46), the reason that Catholics are encouraged to do so is primarily to avoid being condemned to Hell:

When the Son of man shall come in his glory, and all the holy angels with him, then shall he sit upon the throne of his glory:

And before him shall be gathered all nations: and he shall separate them one from another, as a shepherd divideth his sheep from the goats:

And he shall set the sheep on his right hand, but the goats on the left.

Then shall the King say unto them on his right hand, Come, ye blessed of my Father, inherit the kingdom prepared for you from the foundation of the world:

For I was an hungered, and ye gave me meat: I was thirsty, and ye gave me drink: I was a stranger, and ye took me in:

Naked, and ye clothed me: I was sick, and ye visited me: I was in prison, and ye came unto me.

Then shall the righteous answer him, saying, Lord, when saw we thee an hungered, and fed thee? or thirsty, and gave thee drink?

When saw we thee a stranger, and took thee in? or naked, and clothed thee?

Or when saw we thee sick, or in prison, and came unto thee?

And the King shall answer and say unto them, Verily I say unto you, Inasmuch as ye have done it unto one of the least of these my brethren, ye have done it unto me.

Then shall he say also unto them on the left hand, Depart from me, ye cursed, into everlasting fire, prepared for the devil and his angels:

For I was an hungered, and ye gave me no meat: I was thirsty, and ye gave me no drink:

I was a stranger, and ye took me not in: naked, and ye clothed me not: sick, and in prison, and ye visited me not.

Then shall they also answer him, saying, Lord, when saw we thee an hungered, or athirst, or a stranger, or naked, or sick, or in prison, and did not minister unto thee?

Then shall he answer them, saying, Verily I say unto you, Inasmuch as ye did it not to one of the least of these, ye did it not to me.

And these shall go away into everlasting punishment: but the righteous into life eternal.

In this sense, Catholic practice can be seen as irretrievably self-seeking – *the most important thing is that I and my fellow travelers make it to Paradise.*

By contrast, many Protestant sects propose that God freely provides the grace by which alone the faithful believer can be saved. The path to salvation is a sincere profession of faith –

no action is required, because, as the prophet Isaiah says (Chapter 64, verse 6):

But we are all as an unclean thing, and all our righteousnesses are as filthy rags; and we all do fade as a leaf; and our iniquities, like the wind, have taken us away.

The apostle Paul takes up this refrain in Romans (Chapter 3, Verses 10 – 12)

<u>As it is written, There is none righteous, no, not one:</u>

<u>There is none that understandeth, there is none that seeketh after God.</u>

<u>They are all gone out of the way, they are together become unprofitable; there is none that doeth good, no, not one.</u>

However, the redeemed believer will find himself doing good works instinctively, due to the access of divine grace. Hence, virtuous acts are proof of sanctity, rather than a requirement for salvation.

Breaking the cycle

On the other hand, Hinduism and Buddhism see the circle as the emblem of the human condition. The eventual aim is to escape the rounds of birth and death by translation to a state in which the dualities necessitated by personal choices are seen as undulations in a cosmic flux. There is no bifurcation of the cosmos into celestial and infernal regions divided by an impassable gulf. Of course, there are localities in the universe in which the predominant spirit is one of either harmony or disharmony, but these are temporary habitations that emerge from the Void and are later reabsorbed back into it. There is no salvation because there is nothing to be saved from – apart from our ignorance. Once realization is achieved, one returns, like the Prodigal Son, to the "home of the Father" – to the generating consciousness of the Universe –realizing that it is her true home, from which she can never be barred.

At the end of his poem *Little Gidding*, T. S. Eliot gives a description of the "spiritual path" which captures poignantly the human search for personal identity;

> *What we call the beginning is often the end*
> *And to make and end is to make a beginning.*
> *The end is where we start from.*

> *We shall not cease from exploration*
> *And the end of all our exploring*
> *Will be to arrive where we started*
> *And know the place for the first time.*
> *Through the unknown, unremembered gate*
> *When the last of earth left to discover*
> *Is that which was the beginning……..*

Like the soul in Greek mythology drinking of the twin streams of Lethe and Eunoe, memories are first obliterated and then restored – but purely as memories, the soul viewing them like images flitting across a screen. Once the screen is dismantled, the images disappear, but that which is capable of viewing them remains.

Sin

All human beings make mistakes – we are prone to error. In fact, we acquire skills by attempting an activity and finding out how *not* to do it. The child may fall many times while learning to walk, but such errors are accepted as a natural part of the learning process. If we persist in erroneous practices in daily life, experience will usually provide corrective warnings, often painful.

However, when it comes to ethics and morality, the process of learning is much more complicated. The development of a moral sense requires cultivation of an awareness of how our actions will affect not only ourselves, but also those around us and society at large. Therefore, many people and institutions have a vested interest in a child's moral education, and in the establishment of particular moral codes in society.

The origin of sin – a theory

Sin appears to have had its origin in the awareness of environmental enmity, created by forces opposing the wishes or well-being of the individual or tribe. In early human cultures, life was short, brutish, and attended by many dangers. Almost at any time, a man could be plucked out of existence by attack – from a predator or an opposing tribe – or by a force of nature like a flood or a bushfire. Any entity or force that threatened a person's well-being could be interpreted as malevolent. Because such forces appeared to have will and agency, it became natural to imbue them with a degree of personhood, and because of their power, they appeared to have an innate superiority over human beings. Here we have a potential origin of the notion of a deity.

In his book, *The History of the Devil and Idea of Evil*, scholar of comparative religion Paul Carus presents a compelling thesis that the basic religious focus of primitive man was on placating the hostile deities that appeared to control the forces of nature, and that the notion of a benevolent and omnipotent god was a later development. The god of the Pentateuch does appear to be a fractious overlord who is only too eager to visit punishment on people who displease him.

The Persians seem to have been the first religious culture to propose that a good god and an evil one were battling for control of the cosmos, and that the good one would eventually prevail. During the exile of the Jews under Persian rule (586 - 537], this idea came to be incorporated into Judaism and was developed further in Christianity. Eventually, the devil was demoted from his status as a god to that of an evil angel, still powerful but doomed to defeat in the end.

Such perceptions of hostility in the environment would at first probably invite simple opposition, and lead to the development of protective strategies. Then, a realization could have developed that human beings invite disaster by offending a deity, and that future unwelcome events could be forestalled by placating the deity. Hence two concepts emerged that have had a powerful influence on the shaping of society and religion: guilt and reparation.

Guilt

Guilt has two aspects:

- A feeling of remorse at having committed an offence
- An expectation of deserved punishment

While a persistent feeling of guilt may be a punishment in itself, the painful contrition of the offender cannot be expected to relieve any negative feelings or inconvenience suffered by the wounded party. Therefore, strategies have been developed in many cultures to compensate victims of misdeeds. These have taken two basic forms: :

- Gifting – the guilty party deprived himself of something valuable by donating it to the victim
- Atonement – the acceptance of some form of ritual punishment

Gifting

In the Jewish culture of the Old Testament, ritual sacrifice became a primary method of gifting. Sometimes the deity, through prophets, prescribed the offering of sacrifices as a matter of course, somewhat in the manner of a gangster demanding protection money ("Don't want nobody to get 'urt"). An obvious example is in Leviticus 18, verses 1:7-18:

Ye shall bring out of your habitations two wave loaves of two tenth deals: they shall be of fine flour; they shall be baken with leaven; they are the first fruits unto the Lord.

And ye shall offer with the bread seven lambs without blemish of the first year, and one young bullock, and two rams: they shall be for a burnt offering unto the Lord, with their meat offering, and their drink offerings, even an offering made by fire, of sweet savour unto the Lord.

Here it is clear that the Lord would only be satisfied with the very best, and that presenting second-rate offerings could constitute a further offence.

Occasionally, an enterprising soul would attempt to ensure success in an endeavour by striking a sacrificial deal with the Lord in advance, as in the case of Jephthah (Judges 11:30 -31):

And Jephthah vowed a vow unto the Lord, and said, If thou shalt without fail deliver the children of Ammon into mine hands,

Then it shall be, that whatsoever cometh forth of the doors of my house to meet me, when I return in peace from the children of Ammon, shall surely be the Lord's, and I will offer it up for a burnt offering.

Jephthah's military campaign was successful, but unfortunately, the first living thing to greet him on his return home was his daughter, who had rushed out to welcome home the returning hero. Being a man of his word, Jephthah duly but reluctantly committed her to the funeral pyre (Judges 11:39):

And it came to pass at the end of two months, that she returned unto her father, who did with her according to his vow which he had vowed.

In Book Three of the *Aeneid* (translated by John Dryden), the Trojan hero Aeneas seeks to ensure a safe voyage by very generous sacrifices to the gods:

Let us the land which Heav'n appoints, explore;

Appease the winds, and seek the Gnossian shore.

If Jove assists the passage of our fleet,

The third propitious dawn discovers Crete.'

Thus having said, the sacrifices, laid

On smoking altars, to the gods he paid:

A bull, to Neptune an oblation due,

Another bull to bright Apollo slew;

A milk-white ewe, the western winds to please,

And one coal-black, to calm the stormy seas.

Atonement

When Hernán Cortés invaded Mexico in 1519, he discovered that the local Aztec culture had a tradition of extensive ritual human sacrifice. According to Aztec religious doctrine, the gods maintained the universe by continual sacrifice, and hence the Aztecs had the obligation to reciprocate. Scholars disagree on the actual number of sacrificial deaths, but it appears to have numbered in the tens of thousands. The Aztecs also subjected a wide variety of animals to ritual sacrifice. Cortés, in the process of dismantling the Aztec civilization, was able to put a stop to what he saw as a barbaric heathen practice.

Ironically, Christianity is also built around the theme of assuaging the wrath of God by the willing acceptance of punishment. In early Biblical times, when Israel was largely an agrarian society, finding animals to sacrifice was not difficult. However, sacrificial ritual had to be conducted in the correct manner, and hence the profession of priest as interlocuter between man and God developed. As more people moved to cities and could not be expected to have an animal on hand to sacrifice when required, alternative means were needed for satisfying the debt to the ever-demanding deity. Hence, the origin of what has become tithing, whereby the believer could make a convenient and "non-bloody" contribution to the sacrificial endeavour. In the Roman Catholic Church, this is enshrined in the Fifth Commandment of the Catholic Church (Catholic Encyclopedia, 1913): "to contribute to the support of our pastors." Any infraction of any Commandment of the Catholic Church is a mortal sin, which, if not absolved before death, will condemn a person to Hell.

The human proclivity for offending God led to the supposition that sin might be an integral part of human nature rather than just social clumsiness or ignorance. The doctrine of "original sin" proposes an archetypal ancestor who offended the creator so grievously that a permanent stain was placed on his soul, and inclined him to habitual undesirable acts. Even if original sin is washed away in the waters of Christian baptism, humanity's tendency to misbehave remains – we are always potential victims of our innate bad intentions. The propagation of these beliefs has led to the proliferation of explanatory doctrines and corrective procedures and greatly increased clerical power.

It is understandable that people would begin to wonder if there was some ultimate sacrificial act that would resolve God's anger once and for all, and put an end to messy and repetitive rituals of atonement. The idea of a permanent atonement became a notable feature of a new religious cult which became popular during the reign of Augustus, and Paul the Apostle proclaimed (1 Corinthians 15:3)

For I delivered unto you first of all that which I also received, how that Christ died for our sins according to the scriptures.

Jesus became to be seen as the final and perfect sacrifice, the gift of the Creator himself, who in his great (though not infinite) mercy – and perhaps tired of administering severe punishment on anyone who displeased him – collaborated by offering the perfect victim: his own son.

So, one might suppose that a perfect reconciliation between God and humanity had been achieved, and thenceforth God's anger would evaporate and he would regard humans like an indulgent grandparent playing with his grandchildren. Well – not quite. Humankind's nature still contained an intrinsic flaw, the fallout from the "original sin" which had been inherited from our Biblical progenitors, Adam and Eve. The atonement made by Jesus on the cross made it possible for God to cancel out original sin, but our souls had been marked so that the potential to commit further sins remained. The atonement made it possible for people to get to Heaven, but did not prevent them from committing acts that would send them to Hell.

Thomas Aquinas (*Summa Theologica*, Part Three, Question 50, Article 1) explains the nature of the atonement as follows:

It was fitting for Christ to die. First of all to satisfy for the whole human race, which was sentenced to die on account of sin, according to Genesis chapter 2:17: "In what day soever ye shall eat of it ye shall die the death." Now it is a fitting way of satisfying for another to submit oneself to the penalty deserved by that other. And so Christ resolved to die, that by dying He might atone for us, according to 1 Peter 3:18: "Christ also died once for our sins."

However, Thomas concedes that while historical sin may have been remitted, man's capacity for evil still remained. In his treatise *De Malo*, sin is defined as "nothing of else than a morally bad act, an act not in accord with reason informed by the Divine law" (*Catholic Encyclopedia*, 1913). In the same treatise, evil is defined as "a privation of form or order or due measure." The article on Sin in the Catholic *Encyclopedia* goes on to clarify this definition:

"Evil implies a deficiency in perfection, hence it cannot exist in God, who is essentially good: it is found only in finite beings which are subject to the privation of form or order of measure due to them, and are liable to a decrease of their natural perfection."

Therefore, humans being susceptible to error can still sin and require pardon for their offences. Thomas is insistent that no one gets a free pass (*Summa Theologica*, Part Three, Question 86, Article 2): "It is impossible for an mortal actual sin to be pardoned without penance."

No pain, no pardon.

The issue of the forgiveness of sins is one of the main sources of contention between Catholic and Protestant denominations.

Catholics are taught that sin besmirches the soul, which must be sacramentally cleansed before it can be admitted to the Divine presence. As believers are unable to cease sinning, they are in constant need of absolution. Protestant sects, like Calvinism, affirm the intrinsic moral rottenness of man ("total depravity") and assert that God chooses to disregard rather than wipe out the sins of his elect group of souls.

The birth of crime

As society and social institutions become large and more complex, some codification of law was required to cover potential infractions against fairness and rectitude. Hence, a division was developed between sin and crime. Crime is that which offends the body politic – a secular definition of wrongdoing. Sin is that which offends the deity, and therefore includes behaviour that is in no way injurious to other persons or the natural world.

The earliest surviving institutional legal code is that of the Sumerian King Ur-Nammu of Ur, (2112–2095 BCE). Three centuries later, about 1750 BCE, the most legal code, that of King Hammurabi of Babylon was composed.

Both of these documents include a prologue, where the king traces the passing of power to him from a divine being. However, in the legal provisions, the state, rather than a deity, is the entity assessing the offences and determining punishments. Here, we can see the beginning of the move from scriptural law to the constitutional law which is the basis of jurisprudence in a majority of countries in the world today.

Sins or crimes?

In many societies today, most crimes are considered sinful but not all sins form part of the criminal code. For example, both the Ten Commandments and criminal law in most countries define murder and theft as illegal acts. However, in theocracies, the definitions of crime and sin are more tightly intertwined.

In the world of the Old Testament the cosmic ruler was not the rarefied theological entity of modern Christianity and Islam, but a real person, unseen, but enormously powerful, and prone to take offence at any slight to his dignity. If one committed theft or murder, one injured both a human victim and the moral sensibility of God.

The Bible forbids many forms of behavior that it was felt could endanger the social order, under threat of savage punishment. While certain prohibitions make practical and moral sense (e.g. the prohibition of incest), in other cases the penalty of execution appears, at least to our contemporary sensibilities, excessive. In the Pentateuch, the following offences were deemed to be punishable by death:

- adultery (for a married woman and her lover) (Leviticus 20:10; Deuteronomy 22:22)
- bestiality (Deuteronomy 22:13-29)
- blasphemy (Leviticus 24:16)
- child sacrifice (Leviticus 20:1–3)
- false testimony (Deuteronomy 19:16–19)
- false prophecy (Deuteronomy 18:20)

- promotion of other religions (Deuteronomy 13:7–12)
- male homosexuality (Leviticus 20:13)
- idolatry (Leviticus 20:2)
- incest (Leviticus 18:6–16)
- insubordination to authority (Deuteronomy 17:12)
- lying about one's virginity upon marrying a spouse (Deuteronomy 22:13–21)
- kidnapping (Exodus 21:16)
- licentiousness of a priest's daughter (Leviticus 21:9)
- murder (Exodus 21:12)
- rape committed against a betrothed woman (Deuteronomy 22:25)
- cursing, or rebelling against parental authority (Leviticus 20:9)
- Sabbath-breaking (Numbers 15:32–36)
- touching Mount Sinai while God was giving Moses the Ten Commandments (Exodus 19:9–13)
- witchcraft, divination (Leviticus 20:27)

Islamic scripture specifies the following offences as deserving of the death penalty:

- Adultery (Sahih Muslim 17:4209)
- Apostasy (Sahih Bukhari 9:84:57)
- Blasphemy (Sahih Muslim 19:4436)

- Homosexuality (Sunan Abu Dawud 38:444)
- Missing prayer (Sahih Bukhari 1:11:626)
- Murder (Al-Baqarah 2:178)
- Treason 'mischief-making in the land" (Quran 5:32)
- Witchcraft/sorcery (Jami` at-Tirmidhi 3:15:1460)

Today many countries still have statutes against blasphemy. In the UK, laws banning blasphemy were repealed in 2008 in England and Wales, and in Scotland in 2021, but are still current in Northern Ireland. In Europe, the harshest anti-blasphemy laws can be found in the Italian penal code in which the maximum penalty is three years imprisonment. In Muslim majority countries, laws relating to blasphemy are much more stringent and in Iran, Pakistan, Afghanistan, Brunei, Mauritania and Saudi Arabia, blasphemy remains an offence punishable by death.

Not altogether silly

Some of these apparently archaic prohibitions do have a practical basis. A notable example is homosexuality. The ancient Israelites were a small beleaguered tribe, whose hegemony was regularly threatened by attacks from other tribes. The best way to strengthen a tribe is to increase the population. "As for you, be fruitful and increase in number; multiply on the earth and increase upon it." (Genesis, 9:7) As sexual activity among homosexuals, or wanton spilling of the male seed, would not result in procreation, the tribal rulers would naturally want to discourage such practices. Furthermore, legitimizing homosexuality would make childlessness socially acceptable. As Jehovah was a jealous deity, and claimed to have a special fondness for his chosen people, it is understandable that he would consider anything that prevented it from flourishing to be evil.

Another well-known and probably sensible prohibition related to the consumption of pork. The boar of ancient times was not the well-curated source of meat that he is today. He was a wild beast that grazed on any nutriment that could be found, however foul, and came to be regarded as unclean. It is understandable that tribal elders would discourage anything that might spread disease around the camp.

Posthumous punishment

It is said that two things are inevitable in life: death and taxes.

For the atheist or agnostic, death is usually understood as a permanent termination of life in all aspects. In death, the consciousness of personal identity will evaporate and there will be no mechanism for experiencing further sensations or for suffering consequences for any actions performed during life.

On the other hand, most religions posit the concept of a soul, an immaterial essence that is believed to represent the real core of a person, and which will exist eternally after bodily death. Furthermore, many believe that the soul will be judged for all actions, proper and improper, during life on earth. Accordingly, the focus on offences that touched the individual soul rather than the body politic was amplified. Such offences came to be defined as sins, forms of behavior that attacked the moral sensibilities of the presiding deity. As this notion of "spiritual disease" became widely accepted, procedures and policies for dealing with it were developed, and came to form the raison d'être of Judeo-Christian religious practice. In Judaism and Christianity, such procedures require the involvement of ecclesiastical representatives, intermediaries between the deity and the penitent, leading to the growth and continuing influence of a priesthood.

The Four Last Things

Many Christian and Islamic sects support the doctrine of the Four Last Things:

- Death
- Judgement
- Hell
- Heaven

According to this doctrine, all human beings will be subject to judgement after death to assess whether they will be rewarded with eternal bliss or condemned to everlasting torment.

In the *Four Last Things*, a classic Catholic apologetic text, Capuchin priest Martin von Cochem, (1634-1712) writes of the terror of death and impending judgement:

Above and beyond all that we have hitherto considered as contributing to make death terrible to us, is the thought that we must stand before the judgement seat of God, and give an account of all we have done and left undone.

For if it is very alarming even to fall into the hands of an angry man, how much more terrible will it be to fall into the hands of an omnipotent God! All the saints trembled in anticipation of the sentence that would be passed on them by God, for they well knew how exceedingly severe His judgements are. The Royal Psalmist says "Enter not into judgment with Thy servant, O Lord, for in Thy sight no man living shall be justified" (Psalm 142:2).

It is common for both Christians and Muslims to believe that after the created world is dissolved, there will be a second or final judgement. Von Cochem says:

Jesus Christ, the judge of the living and the dead, who at His first coming appeared upon the earth in all stillness and tranquility, under a gentle and attractive form, will come again the second time to judgment with great majesty and glory.

In a later chapter Von Cochem describes the judicial procedure in the afterlife:

When all those whom Christ has chosen to share with Him His office of Judge shall have taken their seats, His apostles having the precedence of all others, the judgment will commence. It appears from what the Apostle St. Paul says that no person, not even the saints, will be exempted from this ordeal. "We shall all stand before the judgment-seat of Christ." (Romans 14:10)

This standing before the judgment-seat of Christ will fill everyone with fear. No one will be free from it; even the just will feel it to a certain degree, as well as the unhappy sinner.

The final judgement is described as follows in the Koran:

Sura 84 - The Splitting Asunder (translation by J. M. Rodwell)

The Art of Non-Expert Living – Oberon Michaels

When the Heaven shall have split asunder

And duteously obeyed its Lord

And when Earth shall have been stretched out as a plain,

And shall have cast forth what was in her and become empty,

And duteously obeyed its Lord

Then verily, O man, who desirest to reach thy Lord shalt thou meet him.

And he into whose right hand his Book shall be given,

Shall be reckoned with in an easy reckoning,

And shall turn, rejoicing, to his kindred.

But he whose Book shall be given him behind his back

Shall invoke destruction:

But in the fire shall he burn.

For that he lived joyously among his kindred.

Without a thought that he should return to God.

Yea, but his Lord beheld him.

It needs not therefore that I swear by the sunset redness.

And by the night and its gatherings.

And by the moon when at her full,

That from state to state shall ye be surely carried onward.

What then hath come to them that they believe not?

And that when the Koran is recited to them they adore not?

Yea, the unbelievers treat it as a lie.

But God knoweth their secret hatreds:

Let their only tidings be those of painful punishment;

Save to those who believe and do the things that be right.

An unfailing recompense shall be theirs.

The Universalist view, i.e., that all people will eventually be saved, has persisted throughout the history of Christianity. Some commentators have even claimed that influential Church father Origen was a supporter of the view that Hell was only temporary. Certain Bible verses certainly appear to support the contention that salvation will be extended to all people:

And all flesh shall see the salvation of God. (Luke 3:6)

As thou hast given him power over all flesh, that he should give eternal life to as many as thou hast given him. (John 17:2)

For this is good and acceptable in the sight of God our Saviour;

Who will have all men to be saved, and to come unto the knowledge of the truth.

For there is one God, and one mediator between God and men, the man Christ Jesus;

Who gave himself a ransom for all, to be testified in due time. (1 Timothy 2:3–6)

For therefore we both labour and suffer reproach, because we trust in the living God, who is the Saviour of all men, specially of those that believe. (1 Timothy 4:10)

However, mainstream sects have generally, and usually vigorously, condemned such a doctrine as heretical. To his contentious *Encyclical Quanta Cura* (1864) Pope Pius IX appended *The Syllabus of Errors*, a document anathematizing eighty popular propositions which he viewed as false and pernicious. Condemned proposition number 17 is:

Good hope at least is to be entertained of the eternal salvation of all those who are not at all in the true Church of Christ.

Many Protestant sects have also issued similar objections to suggestions that anyone outside of their congregations will be saved.

In summary, it can be said that

- atheists and agnostics believe in one final thing – Death;
- universalists in three final things – Death, Judgement and Heaven;
- many orthodox Christians and Muslims – all four last things.

A different view of sin

All religions speak of sin. However, their approaches differ regarding the source of sin. Christianity attributes bad behaviour to humanity's innate moral delinquency, sometimes aided and abetted by the prince of sinners, Satan. Buddhism, on the other hand, sees ignorance, the third of the *Three Fires*, as the prime cause of all wrongdoing. The Buddhist holds that if a person gains true insight into the human condition, he or she will be filled with boundless compassion, and all desire to perform ill deeds will evaporate. All actions, evil and good, have their inevitable consequences, but as these actions are limited by temporality, their effects will also dissipate over time. There is no extrinsic permanent reward or punishment for any deed; there is no eternal realm where the echo of an action continues to resound indefinitely.

However, Buddhist doctrine does stress that wrongdoers will inevitably suffer the effects of their evil actions. In its opening verses, the seminal Buddhist text *The Dhammapada* (translated by F. Max Müller) issues the following admonitions:

All that we are is the result of what we have thought: it is founded on our thoughts, it is made up of our thoughts. If a man speaks or acts with an evil thought, pain follows him, as the wheel follows the foot of the ox that draws the carriage.

All that we are is the result of what we have thought: it is founded on our thoughts, it is made up of our thoughts. If a man speaks or acts with a pure thought, happiness follows him, like a shadow that never leaves him.

In the final chapter, *The Dhammapada* designates the fully evolved being as a *Brahmana*:

Him I call indeed a Brahmana who knows his former abodes, who sees heaven and hell, has reached the end of births, is perfect in knowledge, a sage, and whose perfections are all perfect.

Hence the Buddhist prefers to speak of liberation rather than salvation. The highest state is one in which a person is freed from the shackles of habitual destructive behaviour – in which he or she perceives, not that the soul has been made perfectly clean, but that there never was an enduring soul to be cleansed.

Worship

Worship is usually defined as an act of tendering respect or love for a deity. Sometimes, the term is used to describe veneration offered to a lesser entity, such as a person or a "false idol." In any case, it denotes an active acknowledgment of a being who is:

- Extremely powerful
- Worthy of boundless love
- Infinitely wise
- Free from any imperfection
- Entitled to acknowledgment and service

Accordingly, the object of worship is considered to be sacred. i.e. flawless and not subject to any form of critical evaluation. Ironically, "sacred" is an anagram of "scared": piety is often founded on fear of punishment from a deity who would take offence at being ignored or having his commandments disregarded.

Hence, worship, in this narrow sense, can be seen as reverence personalized. In religious worship, there is an assumption of the exclusivity of the worshipped entity and the need for the devotee to accord continuous acknowledgment. The capacity of the person to render appreciation has to be focused on a single target: the presiding deity, who is the sole source of personal validation.

As Jesus says in the Gospel of John 14:6–7:

I am the way, the truth, and the life: no man cometh unto the Father, but by me.

If ye had known me, ye should have known my Father also: and from henceforth ye know him, and have seen him.

In other words, "my way or the highway."

Feeling 'worshipful'

I propose that rendering reverence is a much more universal human trait than the approach suggested above, and that worship can be more broadly and healthily defined. A person may be committed to a worthwhile activity, a principle, or a noble cause, and derive a satisfaction and feeling of empowerment comparable to those of the nervous, worshipping pew-dweller. Religious apologists often claim that those who lack faith are trapped in a barren world of materialism and have no understanding of the joy and empowerment that comes from the practice of genuine religion. According to them, nothing can compare to the delight and sense of personal enhancement that come from diligent prostration to a conceptual deity of uncertain temper.

The newly born-again Christian may state that he feels that he has come alive by allowing Jesus to enter his soul. What has actually happened is the stimulation of a new and uplifting feeling, which the person sees as the result of adopting his new faith and the resulting indwelling of Christ's Spirit. Similarly, the pious Catholic may experience a certain sense of psychological renewal after leaving the confessional booth. In both cases, the experience is subjective, built on the person's expectation of positive benefit. In visceral terms, it may be compared to the intense relief one may feel on narrowly avoiding a serious accident or on hearing that a loved one in a theatre of war has escaped to safety. In each of these cases, the prime cause of relief is a relaxation of fear and an enhanced feeling of certainty.

Expanding worship

If we expand the definition of worship to include reverence for that which makes us more functional, joyful and empowered, we see that it can be widely applied in daily life. Let us take the hypothetical case of John, a keen philatelist (postage stamp collector). He is upright and honest, and is happily married with three children. The entire family is heavily invested in philately, in which John is an acknowledged expert. In his house, he has an inner sanctum, in which his stamps are securely stored, and on the walls of which some of his favourite specimens are displayed. He is highly ethical in his dealings with other philatelists, with whom he forms a large community that is very supportive of its members, treating them like extended family. He is fascinated by all aspects of stamps, their manufacture and use; he finds pleasure in investigating the machinery used to print stamps in earlier times; he ponders on the power of a small piece of decorative paper to enable communication across the world and to enable commerce. However, his greatest delight is in examining a rare specimen very closely, marveling at the compelling quality of the artwork. This he can do for hours on end, in a state of blissful introspection.

Neither John nor any member of his family is religious. However, through his passionate pursuit, John has enjoyed many of the benefits that organized religion is said to offer:

- powerful community support
- a deep feeling of belonging
- appreciation of beauty
- understanding of order
- ethical behaviour
- intellectual discipline

Many non-religious communities function much more harmoniously than religious groups. The construction of the Large Hadron Collider, the largest physics project ever conceived, required the cooperation of a vast body of qualified personnel, drawn from many different countries. Other ambitious projects like the building of long bridges or massive skyscrapers require the effective cooperation of many people. Successful completion of such projects is dependent on an abiding non-sectarian respect for the worth of the enterprise and the people collaborating on it. However, one is not expected to offer extravagant homage to the supervising architect or engineer, or to lavishly praise the generosity of the company that provided the finance.

We can eschew religious worship quite safely without losing our inclination for respect for principles and people, our appreciation of beauty, or our sense of awe. Everyone, believer or non-believer, can marvel at the evocative charm of a beautiful melody, the stupendous glories of the night sky, the intricate structure of insect societies, or the mysterious complexities of the human body.

Liberation

Broadly speaking, the purpose of spiritual practice is to free the devotee from the limitations of phenomenal existence.

Christianity proposes that the limiting factor is sin and the consequences that flow from it. Failure to attain God-given freedom causes not only unfortunate repercussions in this life, but also eternal punishment in the afterlife.

By contrast, Hinduism and Buddhism present the view that the failure to attain liberation entails ongoing suffering in this world, but that the suffering will be resolved permanently when the practitioner achieves final realization. Punishment relates to specific evil acts, and ceases when the consequences of the acts are worked out, and the desire to behave in undesirable ways is extirpated.

The forgiveness of sin

Let us take the procedures of the Roman Catholic Church as a typical Christian method of resolving the issues flowing from sin. To have sins forgiven, one must obtain absolution from a priest in the sacramental ritual of confession. If a person dies with any major sins unforgiven, he or she will be condemned to hell.

Five steps can be identified in this highly bureaucratic process:

1. Awareness
2. Contrition
3. Confession – admission
4. Forgiveness
5. Penance

The penitent must first become aware of his moral failures, and this is done by what is called an *examination of conscience*. He considers the events of his daily life since his last confession, and identifies the occasion when he has sinned. He should then feel deep sorrow for having offended God, and enter the confessional booth in that remorseful mood.

The Catholic catechism has an extremely extensive list of sins, which may be divided into two groups: *venial* or *minor*, and *mortal* or *grave*. Mortal sin blocks the soul from access to divine grace and leads to damnation if absolution is not received – in other words, the soul becomes as if dead. It is stressed that most of the time, no person is free from sin and cannot expect to cease sinning.

After hearing the confession, the priest, in most cases, gives absolution and gives a penance. This is usually the recitation of a small number of prayers. The person can then leave the church, resplendent in the glow of conscious sinlessness.

Martin Luther's initial point of discontent with the Roman Church was not the sale of indulgences, but the issue of confession. Luther was an obsessive penitent, plaguing his confessors with extravagant recitals of his failings, and seeking absolution as soon as he suspected that he had committed a further sin. Unable to shake the constant awareness of his innate sinfulness, he researched scripture for some relief and arrived at the solution that man would always be infested with sin, and hence the constant practice of confession would not change his status as a habitual wrongdoer. The source of spiritual regeneration was not priestly absolution, but rather the grace of God, by which the guilt of sin is borne by Christ through his atoning sacrifice on the cross. The followers of John Calvin codified the relevant principles as "total depravity" (man's innate moral delinquency) and "limited atonement" (the clearing of sinfulness by Christ from true believers).

In any case, spiritual realization means the acceptance of sin by the believer and his vicarious salvation by the action of a divine third party.

A different model

I agree that awareness of sin is an indication of essential human fallibility and the wish to achieve an ideal state of being. However, I believe that this internal discontent has a neurological and social basis, and that religious practice is not an effective way of resolving it.

The five steps in the process that I suggest are as follows:

1) Repulsion

2) Admission

3) Expiation

4) Forgiveness

5) Release

Repulsion

Disgust is a familiar sensation to most people and results in feelings of revulsion and avoidant behaviour. Such feelings can be tracked to activity in the left amygdala, the left inferior frontal cortex, and the insular cortex within the human brain. When the feeling becomes very intense, it can lead to phobias, which can be terrifying and can impose severe limits in daily life.

My theory is that disgust can be equated to the perception of sin, in that it is a permanent source of internal unpleasantness. The patterns of habitual disgust are established early in life, and thus can be seen as a fixed aspect of the personality. If we are encouraged to see the imperfections that we perceive in our environment as a reflection of our own moral shortcomings, then we can be persuaded that the fault is in ourselves.

However, the reasonable view is that we are not responsible for most of the general unpleasantness that we encounter in daily life. Our bodies produce unattractive waste, which we prefer to dispose of in a way that does not arouse disgust. Disease can render the human form both toxic and hideous. But when someone contracts cancer, the cause may be assumed to be the behaviour of some rogue genes, rather than a structural 'yuckiness' in the person. Similarly, it is not reasonable that the visitations of major catastrophes of nature, like the tsunami in the Pacific region in 2004, have their source in the errant qualities of the inhabitants of those localities.

Admission

The first action required is acceptance of the unpleasant element in a situation. A problem must first be acknowledged before it can be addressed.

Expiation

In the Roman Catholic confessional model, expiation follows forgiveness; in the alternative model, the steps are reversed. Expiation is corrective or compensatory action. If the thief wishes to be considered reformed, he must cease stealing and, to the best of his ability, make restitution to his victims. There may be tender-hearted souls who are willing to offer forgiveness to an offending party without evidence of reform, but there is usually at least an expectation that the evil-doer will correct his ways. However, if the guilty party promises to current his behaviour, without any intention of actually doing so, this would be deceit and the corrective process would be null and void.

Forgiveness

The best definition of forgiveness that I have heard is "giving up the desire to punish:" advice given to me by a close friend when I was the victim of an extreme act of betrayal. By contrast, the religious definition is the action of God in either wiping the stain of sin from the soul (Catholicism) or disregarding it (Calvinism). Releasing the desire to punish an offending party is psychologically nourishing to both offender and victim. Such forgiveness is very practical. It does not require that the victim come to like the offender, or indeed continue to associate with him. But it does prevent the offender and his misdeeds from renting space in the victim's consciousness and allows the victim to move on with his life.

Release

This is the state represented by the Greek myth of drinking from the rivers of Lethe and Eunoe. The impact of the nefarious deed is reduced to a blip, an occasional reminiscence that may be recalled by the victim without trauma.

Victimhood

The above use of the term "victim" is not restricted to the person who is the target of a vicious or unkind action. In a sense, all participants are victims of any action which causes damage. An external operator is not necessarily required; addiction or over-indulgences are cases in which the victim and the perpetrator are the same person.

In his classic self-help monograph, *As A Man Thinketh*, James Allen describes the complications which arise in the generally accepted categorization of wrong-doers and victims:

It has been usual for men to think and to say, "Many men are slaves because one is an oppressor; let us hate the oppressor." Now, however, there is amongst an increasing few a tendency to reverse this judgment, and to say, "One man is an oppressor because many are slaves; let us despise the slaves." The truth is that oppressor and slave are co-operators in ignorance, and, while seeming to afflict each other, are in reality afflicting themselves.

Final destination

Relief from sin and its immediate effects can be seen as a conditional form of liberation. However, it is a universal desire to graduate to a state where one is permanently free from all impediments.

The ultimate aim of the Christian or Muslim devotee might be to obtain a place in a posthumous paradise. The aim of the Buddhist adherent is instead to achieve a condition of beatitude in which all opposites are resolved in immersion in a blissful cosmic unity.

After death, the Christian goes to a place, a location that suggests definite geographical properties. Some apologists and pastors teach that Hell is an actual subterranean region, like that depicted in *Dante's Inferno*. Heaven and Hell are separated by an impassable gulf, as described in the Parable of Dives and Lazarus (Luke 16:22–31). As the narrative indicates, the blessed can look over the fence, behold the damned writhing in torment below, and communicate with them.

And it came to pass, that the beggar died, and was carried by the angels into Abraham's bosom: the rich man also died, and was buried;

And in hell he lift up his eyes, being in torments, and seeth Abraham afar off, and Lazarus in his bosom.

And he cried and said, Father Abraham, have mercy on me, and send Lazarus, that he may dip the tip of his finger in water, and cool my tongue; for I am tormented in this flame.

But Abraham said, Son, remember that thou in thy lifetime receivedst thy good things, and likewise Lazarus evil things: but now he is comforted, and thou art tormented.

And beside all this, between us and you there is a great gulf fixed: so that they which would pass from hence to you cannot; neither can they pass to us, that would come from thence.

Then he said, I pray thee therefore, father, that thou wouldest send him to my father's house:

For I have five brethren; that he may testify unto them, lest they also come into this place of torment.

Abraham saith unto him, They have Moses and the prophets; let them hear them.

And he said, Nay, father Abraham: but if one went unto them from the dead, they will repent.

And he said unto him, If they hear not Moses and the prophets, neither will they be persuaded, though one rose from the dead.

In the *Summa Theologica* (Third Part, Supplement, Question 94), Thomas Aquinas provides the following explanation:

In order that the happiness of the saints may be more delightful to them and that they may render more copious thanks to God for it, they are allowed to see perfectly the sufferings of the damned. So that they may be urged the more to praise God. The saints in heaven know distinctly all that happens to the damned.

A corollary of Aquinas' approach is the idea that the blessed are able to mock the damned and would be justified in doing so.

In Cantos 32 and 33 of the *Inferno*, Dante describes how he applies the uncharitable approach of Aquinas to the unfortunate souls who are submerged up to the neck in the frozen ground of the Ninth Circle. Canto 32 describes how Dante, as he stumbles across the ice, happens to kick the head of one of the sinners, who, unsurprisingly, cries out in protest. Dante demands the name and history of the complaining soul, and begins to torture him by ripping out his hair when he refuses to comply. Fortunately for the victim of this abuse, another condemned sinner calls him by his name and Dante recognizes him. After Dante releases his grip, the damned soul names those around him who are sharing his misery.

In Canto 33, Dante has a conversation with the traitorous Friar Alberigo. As the friar weeps, his tears turn to ice which becomes encrusted around his eyes. He offers to talk to Dante, on condition that the poet will afterwards brush the ice from his face. At the end of the conversation, the Friar says: "But now stretch out hither thy hand; open my eyes for me." Dante's response? "And I opened them not for him, and to be rude to him was courtesy." (From the translation by Charles Eliot Norton.)

The Koran also contains many descriptions of Hell and the specific torments that will be inflicted there (suras 2:24, 2:161-162, 2:176, 4:52, 4:55-56, 5:36-37, 14;16, 22:19-22, 37:62-68, 44:43-46, 55:44, 101:8-11).

Hence, the spiritual ambition of the Christian or Muslim devotee is salvation from eternal punishment, rather than liberation. Dwellers in the afterlife are the subjects of a rigid autocracy, benign for those in Heaven and ghastly for those in Hell. Furthermore, unlike political tyrannies, this disposition of ruling power will be eternal and unchanging.

By contrast, the spiritual aspirant of the East seeks enlightenment or liberation, i.e. elevation to a state in which there is no power structure, but union with all that is. Physical death does not guarantee admission to this realm. Whether a definable state of afterlife exists or is personally accessible is a secondary consideration – the major focus should be on dealing with the challenges of life in the phenomenal world.

The Pathless Path

One of the most significant texts in Zen literature is a long poem attributed to the third Chinese Patriarch, *Seng T'san* (d. 606 BCE), entitled "On Faith in the Heart." In simple verbiage, he describes the essentially circular structure of life in the world of phenomena, and reveals the way to escape the snares of duality.

The poem consists of thirty-one stanzas, from which the following selection has been made, from the translation made by Buddhist scholar, D. T. Suzuki.

    1.   The Perfect Way knows no difficulties
          Except that it refuses to make preferences;
          Only when freed from hate and love,
          It reveals itself fully and without disguise;
          A tenth of an inch's difference,
          And heaven and earth are set apart;
          If you wish to see it before your own eyes,

Have no fixed thoughts either for or against it.

2. To set up what you like against what you dislike –
   This is the disease of the mind:
   When the deep meaning of the Way is not understood
   Peace of Mind is disturbed to no purpose.

3. The Way is perfect like unto vast space,
   With nothing wanting, nothing superfluous:
   It is indeed due to making choice
   That its suchness is lost sight of.

4. Purse not the outer entanglements,
   Dwell not in the inner void;
   Be serene in the oneness of things,
   And dualism vanishes by itself.

30. One in All,
    All in One -
    If only this is realized,
    No more worry about your not being perfect!

31. Where Mind and each believing mind are not divided,
    And undivided are each believing mind and Mind,
    This is where words fail;
    For it is not of the past, present, and future.

The path that the patriarch is describing is the same as that referred to by T. S. Eliot in his immortal lines in Little Gidding:

> *...the end of all our exploring*
> *Will be to arrive where we started*
> *And know the place for the first time.*

In *Everybody's Autobiography* (1937), Gertrude Stein remarked about her demolished childhood home in Oakland:

> *There is no there there.*

Following the Patriarch's lead we could add the paraphrase:

> *There is no here here.*

In other words, no seeking is required to find the Path – we are already on it. Just take care to avoid the snares.

The Art of Non-Expert Living – Oberon Michaels

Chapter 4: Strategies

A menu of options

To address the demands of life, one must develop right understanding and then use that to formulate and direct right action. (Remember, 'right' here is not a matter of what is absolutely correct or not wrong; rather it is what is most appropriate or fitting to a particular context).

In this section, we will look at strategies that I have found helpful in the management of daily life. Few of these are original, and none of them require extreme application.

A popular view of great success is that it demands dramatic expression of the remarkable. However, those who are considered masters of any discipline usually find the exercise of their particular skill normal and unexceptional.

What drives us?

As was stated in the introduction to this book, I have always had a particular interest in people who have worked things out "from first principles."

One such person was Lester Levenson, a physicist, engineer and entrepreneur, who in 1952 was diagnosed with terminal coronary heart disease. Levenson, who was 42 at the time, had endured many years of chronic illness, both physical and psychological. After being told to go home and prepare for his death, he decided to plunge into a deep examination of the meaning of life. After three months of intense introspection, he came to certain realizations about the mind, and in the process achieved complete bodily healing. He remained active and in good health until his passing in 1994.

Levenson codified his discoveries in what has become known as the *Sedona Method*, named after the city in Arizona which has since become known as a Mecca for all things New Age. The Method is a system of internal questioning, which is simple but surprisingly effective if applied rigorously. This book does not teach the Method, which can be learned from books and audio courses published by Sedona Training Associates, or from a trained instructor. However, there is a particular element of the method which can be very useful in helping to understand the motivations and actions of ourselves and others. Levenson proposed three primary drivers behind every action or expression of emotion:

- Desire for control
- Desire for approval
- Desire for security

Using this template, we can establish a useful guide for evaluating people (including ourselves) and their actions.

While each of these desires is active in each person, in most cases one of the three will have predominance. Identifying the primary desire or driver can provide valuable insights into character.

Desire for Control

The person in whom this desire is paramount is most likely to be a leader or a fighter. When the desire is expressed in excess, the person will become a tyrant. When it is well regulated, the person will more likely be a leader who is calm in crisis, able to meet difficult situations effectively, and provides useful support and guidance to others.

For such a person, a difficulty is a challenge rather than a hindrance – an obstacle to be countered and overcome, rather than a sentence of incapacity.

Desire for approval

This desire can be very debilitating. Approval can be sought from two sources:

1. Other people
2. Circumstances

Chronic dependence on the approval of others is very disempowering. It deals a severe blow to any sense of self-esteem and can inhibit the ability to make appropriate choices. It is an attitude inevitably fostered by cults, and in essence, creates a state of emotional slavery.

The person whose primary drive is for control will confront and attempt to overcome unfavorable circumstances; the person who requires approval will often see an adverse event as an insuperable obstacle, and the failure to deal with it as a crushing personal judgement.

The desire to make others happy is praiseworthy, but can be destructive if one's prime intention is to gain approval from another. In some cases, truly helping a person can mean going against their immediate wishes.

Desire for security

Life is ever uncertain and it is prudent to make sensible provision for possible adverse events. Actions like taking out insurance policies, accumulating savings, and observing commonly applied health practices are important and reasonable.

Similarly, the maintenance of solid family and social networks is an essential aspect of a well-functioning society.

Another positive aspect of this desire is the development and support of humanitarian endeavours. It is inspiring to witness and work with groups of people who are working together to create a safer and more flourishing world.

The negative application of this desire results in a fearful and closeminded relationship with the outside world. People who are overconcerned with security can become extremely cautious and also very mistrustful of other people and their intentions. They can become obsessed with the possibilities of future disasters, personal or societal. In general, conspiracy theorists are dominated by this desire.

The Whole Person

No person is dominated by just one of the primary desires. What needs to be considered is the order of dominance of each desire.

The following template, which is purely my own creation, is intended to be a useful guide for estimating the concomitant mixture of all three desires.

Desire ranking			Application	
Primary	**Secondary**	**Tertiary**	**Positive**	**Negative**
Control	Approval	Security	Activist	Narcissist
Control	Security	Approval	Protector	Tyrant
Approval	Control	Security	Motivator	Preacher
Approval	Security	Control	Empath	Sycophant
Security	Control	Approval	Regulator	Sociopath
Security	Approval	Control	Investigator	Conspirator

Of course, human motivation is a far more complex issue than can be described/exhausted/circumscribed with a recipe for mixing primary desires. However, establishing a person's dominant desire can be very useful in evaluating the underlying motivation of any action, as well as the methods a person uses to achieve desired results.

What can we do about our own motivations?

Can we decide to change the desire which is the prime driver of our attitudes and our actions? Well, we can decide that we would like to, but as our lives are largely governed by our neurology and memories of our lived experience, the process is not as simple as flicking a switch. However, once we have determined the desire t is most influential in our lives, we can start to reorganize our daily routines to minimize exposure to the situations we find most debilitating. We can also use this approach as an aid for determining strategies to help us respond effectively in challenging situations.

The Three Modes of Choice

Choices are generally governed by necessity, or more accurately, by the perception of necessity. Human beings cannot refrain from action – even remaining immobile can be seen as a form of action! So, life is a cascade of actions. Such actions are prompted by choices.

In examining our decisions, it is helpful to explore the impetus or driving force in the decision, before considering the outcome.

Here is a basic template whereby actions can be categorized as *should–would–could*.

Should

These actions are driven primarily by social or religious expectations. The incentives for such action are usually based on fear of retribution or withdrawal of favour as a result of non-compliance. The most obvious example is attending to religious obligations to avoid hell. Another instance is a child undertaking a course of study to retain a parent's approval.

In many cases, these actions are performed unwillingly and in a spirit of powerful resentment. Even if the action is itself beneficial, the doer is unlikely to perform it in an optimal fashion, or appreciate the benefits that may accrue, because of the sense that the choice is dominated by another's agency above their own.

The use of the past conditional form "should have" actually indicates that the desired action has not been performed, or the desired outcome has not been achieved.

Would

These are actions that can be performed easily, frequently, and without notable personal effort.

Obviously, the content of this category is peculiarly personal. For the captain of a 747, landing a plane at an airport on a calm day may be unremarkable and a typical activity of his daily life. On the other hand, for a terrified untrained passenger who has to guide the plane down in an emergency, the event is both incredibly demanding and very memorable.

If you examine the content of your daily routine, you will observe that many activities fall into this 'would' category – getting out of bed, brushing your teeth, traveling to work, and making phone calls. For the majority of people, these activities require neither training nor great effort, nor do they invoke an extreme emotional state like fear or anger. However, the humdrum nature of an activity does not mean that it might not be challenging for some people, for example, for those who suffer from some form of phobia. There are people who are otherwise fully functional in life and who have such a severe fear of heights that they find it very difficult to climb a short ladder.

In summary, the "would" category is comprised of those actions which are seen as totally unremarkable to the doer, and which are performed frequently or habitually.

Could

This category includes actions that are possible for the doer to perform, but which would require special effort, training, and in certain cases, supervision. The doer may have the resources and the opportunity to perform the action, but require significant stimulation, support, and personal effort to complete the task.

Such events are often remarkable for the person themselves, although they may not be perceived as remarkable in the broader community. For example, the performance of a complicated piano concerto by a young pianist at his or her first public appearance may be felt by the executant to be a remarkable and challenging event, while a public performance of the same work by a seasoned virtuoso in a nearby city could be experienced as "another day at the office."

Actions excluded from this are those that a person has no reasonable expectation of performing. For example, if you have never taken a swimming lesson, have never visited the beach or a swimming pool, and have a low level of physical fitness, to state that you intend to swim the English Channel next week is clearly unreasonable. On the other hand, if you gradually took all the required steps over an appropriate period of time, you could work up to achieving this feat, as did author and media personality David Walliams. The intermediate steps fall into the 'would' category. Hence the steps to the remarkable are an extended series of 'woulds.' The thousand-mile journey starts with a single step.

Summary

Should – what you feel that you ought to do.

Would – what you do as a matter of course.

Could – what you may be capable of, given inspiration and opportunity.

Things to remember:

In the immortal words of the prophet Brian Cohen: "You are all individuals." It is senseless to estimate your intrinsic worth by comparing the volume and magnitude of your personal achievements with those of others. There is only one Isaac Newton, Wolfgang Amadeus Mozart, Michael Jordan, Roger Federer or Stephen Hawking. While the accomplishments of these remarkably gifted individuals may be extremely significant, it does not mean the achievements of those with less ability have less value as part of a life journey.

Attitude

In recent years, *attitude* is a term that has come to have a negative connotation. It is commonly used to indicate an aggressive, unpleasant and uncooperative approach to others, and indeed, to life itself. However, the more accurate and universal definition of the term is *a habitual way of thinking about things*. We have all developed opinions on a wide range of issues, and these profoundly affect the way we act and react. So, to change our habitual behaviours, we need to consider our opinions, and hence our attitudes, which can be seen as the projection of our opinions.

I have long been interested in the products and therapies which can be found in the vast self-help market. There is, of course, a lot of material that is fantastical, untested and untestable, or just eccentric. However, the real problem with many self-help therapies is not lack of efficacy, but unwillingness on the part of consumers to practice a chosen therapy with the required diligence. The reaction of many people to a therapeutic call to discipline is like that of a child in a sweet shop – as soon as the novelty of one therapy wears off, they move to another one. For effective application, self-help modalities require thorough practice, just as does developing expertise in sport, music or any other discipline.

At a radio interview with email marketing consultant Telman Knudsen, self-help mentor, T. Harv Eker shared the following wisdom. If you want to improve your life immediately, he advised, you should avoid three negative habits: blaming, complaining and justifying. You should also cultivate the positive habit of celebrating the good fortune of others. These recommendations may seem obvious, but a little examination of one's life will illustrate how rarely they are applied.

Full details of Eker's methods can be found in his book, *Secrets of the Millionaire Mind*.

Eker's recommendations tie in with another maxim much favoured by self-help practitioners:

It is not your fault – but it's your responsibility

Let us examine these habits or attitudes to see how changing them can change our lives.

Blaming

You arrive at your house to find it engulfed in flames. A neighbour rushes up and informs you that arson is suspected. You say, "Well I didn't start the fire – so it's not up to me to do anything about it. They should find the so-and-so who started it and get him to put it out."

A similar instance: You are walking along the footpath when you are struck by a passing car driven at great speed which has strayed from the roadway. The vehicle tears off into the distance without the driver paying you the slightest heed. As you lie on the ground with a broken leg, a passerby approaches and asks if you want help. You reply, "No – the lowlife who was driving that car caused this, so it's up to him to fix it. He's the one who should call the ambulance."

In both cases, most people would say that such an attitude is ridiculous. When confronted with the burning house, the sensible owner would call the fire brigade and offer assistance to any neighbours who were threatened by the fire. If you were the victim of the hit-and-run accident, you would, as a matter of course, seek medical assistance. If later, when visited in hospital by a friend, you are told that the erring driver has been caught and charged, you may feel relief and a sense of justice – but you are still responsible for complying with medical treatment.

While these two cases are extreme examples, it cannot be denied that we place great significance on finding who is at fault in unfortunate events, even when the result is of no consequence to our personal lives. Too often we labour under the delusion that a situation will be resolved by finding the one at fault.

Another function of blame is to feel our own sense of moral superiority. For example, the 'value' of subjecting the rich and influential to moral judgements may enable us to feel morally superior, assuring ourselves that we would *never* behave in such a fashion. By extension, we can then attribute blame to large sectors of the community with whom we happen to disagree, blaming them for the ills that afflict society. Just think of that cartel of faceless 'leftists' who are blamed for everything that is defined as a danger to the social fabric.

The reality is that we are responsible for dealing with what happens in our lives. Whether the hand we are dealt is seen as fair or otherwise, the business of daily living continues unabated. If we focus primarily on finding solutions to problems rather than on finding people to blame, we will function with more efficiency and less tension.

Complaining

Complaining in the sense of the present discussion is a cousin of blame. It is the expression of certain discontent, with the implication that someone else should fix our problem. It is, in essence, an admission of a lack of power, or will, to address an undesirable situation. General complaints about the corruption or inefficiency of large organizations or social groups are included in this category.

Marcus Aurelius gives sage advice for those of us inclined toward this tendency. He divides events into two categories:

- Those that one can control or influence
- Those that are beyond a person's control

His recommendation is that a wise person should attend diligently to those events in the first category and ignore those in the second.

The happiest people are those who see least to complain about in the world. This does not mean that these people do not feel concern about major issues like political oppression, world hunger or natural disasters. Rather, they focus on helping where they can, and avoid belabouring others with expressions of their disappointment with the unfortunate events of an imperfect world.

This Zen parable illustrates an ingenious way of dealing with complaints.

Bankei Yotaku (1622-1693) was one of the most celebrated Zen masters of his time, and was dearly loved by students and local inhabitants alike. One day, a group of monks came to him, complaining that a novice had been caught stealing. They demanded that the master take action against the offender. Bankei did nothing.

Shortly afterwards, the novice was again caught stealing. This time a group of angry monks dragged the delinquent before the master.

"Expel this worthless fellow," they insisted. "If you don't, all of us will leave."

Bankei looked at them sadly, and replied, "You are wise monks; you know the difference between good and evil. But this unfortunate fellow does not know the difference between good and evil. I will keep him here with me, even if all the rest of you leave."

A cascade of tears pouted down the guilty monk's cheeks, and he felt the desire to steal suddenly and permanently disappear.

It is notable that Bankei acknowledged the monks' complaint and addressed the issue without becoming defensive or giving ground.

Justifying

Of the three habits to be avoided, this is possibly the most insidious. Justifying is the manufacture and presentation of excuses, and may arise in one of the following situations:

- When we have done something we feel should not have done
- When we fail to do something expected of us
- When we perform poorly
- When we are threatened with severe punishment

- When we are in an environment where failure is not tolerated.

Justifying often involves shifting the blame to circumstances or other people.

To avoid lapsing into the habit of justifying, frank admission of the faulty behaviour is required. A corollary is that responsibility should also be accepted.

Celebrating good fortune

You win the lottery. Celebrate! A new baby is born in the family. Mother and child are faring very well. Celebrate! Your football team wins a national championship after decades in the doldrums. Celebrate!

Your neighbour wins the lottery; your unpleasant boss reports the happy arrival of a new addition to the family; or the football team that you love to hate wins a championship. You find that you feel little desire to celebrate.

Again, we turn to the life of Bankei for an illustration of how our feelings can be coloured by favourable or unfavourable circumstances.

After Bankei's death, a blind man who lived in a nearby village observed, "Because I am blind, I have learned to judge people by the quality of their speech. When I hear someone congratulating another who has been fortunate, I often detect an undertone of envy or resentment that the good fortune passed the speaker by. Similarly, when a person is commiserating with someone who has suffered a bad turn of fortune, I can often sense a feeling of relief, or even pleasure that the misfortune has happened to someone else. With Zen master Bankei, it was different. When he expressed joy, joy was all I heard; when he expressed sorrow, all I heard was sorrow."

When we are passed up for a promotion, lose a race or suffer some similar negative turn of events, we are often tempted to think resentfully of the person who has been successful. This is the inverse side of the tendency to justify: we try to persuade ourselves that our loss, failure, or embarrassment is really the fault of some external factor – either a person or unfavourable circumstances. Of course, indulging in such a train of thought only makes the emotional wound sharper and more long-lasting.

Eker's advice is to see anything which is genuinely beneficial for a person, and which stimulates that person to rejoice, as being good for everyone in the environment. If you become habituated to seeing the accumulation of wealth, growth in personal popularity, and the accession of good fortune as evidence of favoritism, corruption and injustice, you are blocking the road to your own success and happiness.

Not taking it personally

Often when a person advises you, "Don't take it personally," it is to disguise or excuse some gratuitously unpleasant or harmful action on their part. However, to a degree, "not taking things personally" can be a recipe for countering the deleterious effects of blaming, complaining and justifying.

This story of the famous Zen master Hakuin illustrates the power of such abnegation:

Hakuin was one of the most celebrated Zen masters in Japan. He ran a large monastery with an extensive retinue of students and was regarded as a model of probity. Because of his good reputation and popularity, he attracted considerable aristocratic patronage, and the monastery became a flourishing establishment.

In the neighbouring town, a young unmarried woman was discovered to be pregnant. She came from a wealthy and influential family who were very keen to avoid any form of social embarrassment. Accordingly, they pressed the girl to reveal who the father was. For a long time, she refused to divulge his identity, but just before the birth of the baby she said, "I was seduced by the Zen teacher, Hakuin."

When the child was born, the girl's father, accompanied by a large body of servants, stormed into the monastery and confronted Hakuin. After denouncing him at length as a hypocrite and a shameless abuser of young woman, the father dropped the baby at Hakuin's feet, saying, "You take care of this bastard – after all, it's yours."

Hakuin's only response, as he bent to pick up the infant, was to say, "Is that so?"

Word spread quickly about the Zen master's fall from grace. Many of his students abandoned him, the aristocratic patrons withdrew their support and the monastery fell on hard times.

Hakuin remained serenely unconcerned, and assiduously devoted his attention to the rearing of the child. He would go to the town to beg for milk to feed it and appeared completely impervious to the insults that were heaped on him. Meanwhile, the child flourished in the monastic surroundings and was a picture of health and happiness.

A year passed. Then the mother, racked by guilt and desperately wishing to be reunited with her child, approached her father, and confessed that the real father of the baby was not Hakuin, but a young man who worked at the fish market.

The father exploded with wrath. "Not only did you get yourself pregnant to some nobody who works in a shop, but you also tricked me into maligning the name of a great and good man. I wish to have nothing more to do with you. You are no longer my daughter. Leave this house immediately."

"I will leave – but only if you will do one thing for me. Go with me to the monastery and help me to ask for my baby back," said the girl.

At first, the father refused. However, the girl was so persistent in her demand that eventually he reluctantly acquiesced.

On this occasion, just the girl and the father went to the monastery. As soon as the father saw Hakuin, he threw himself on the ground and begged pardon for the false accusations he had made about the priest's character.

The father's expressions of contrition continued for some time, during which Hakuin remained silent. Eventually, the father mentioned, in an off-hand manner, that the baby's mother had said that she would like to see her child.

"Is that so?" said Hakuin, and immediately handed the baby back to its mother.

Not getting involved

Another aspect of the power of remaining detached in a challenging situation is demonstrated in the following story.

When the Meiji restoration was initiated in Japan in 1868, the Samurai class lost its aristocratic privileges. The result was a protracted rebellion, during which some 50,000 Samurai lost their lives.

During the war, a fugitive Samurai sought sanctuary in a Zen monastery. The abbot concealed him and returned to his practice in the meditation hall.

Shortly afterwards, two officers arrived in pursuit of the fugitive. The abbot disclaimed all knowledge of the man or his whereabouts.

The senior officer drew his sword and said, "I know that rascal is round here somewhere. If you won't tell me, I will cut off your head."

The abbot calmly said, "Oh, if I am going to die, I may as well enjoy some wine first." He picked a bottle that was lying nearby and poured himself a small glass with a completely steady hand. He then sipped the wine in an attitude of calm detachment.

The officers looked at each other and then at the abbot. Eventually, the senior officer sheathed his sword, and the two men silently left the premises.

The abbot was asked many times to comment on this incident, but for a long time refused to say anything. He was finally persuaded to make the following observation:

"These two men burst in and demanded to know where the Samurai was. I did not oppose them, but merely stayed in my world and allowed them to remain in theirs. After a while, I discovered that they had gone away."

Your attitude or your life

When I considered the effect of abandoning these judgmental habits, it struck me that if everyone avoided them, the new media would be stripped of much of its content. On a surface level, life would appear to be robbed of much of its colour. For example, in television soap operas, warring couples are seen as much more interesting than those who live in harmony, and consequently, the fighters get much more air time than the lovers.

However, if we want to gain insight into the true nature of personality, we must plunge deep below the fluctuating surface of popular scandal. There is a beauty, a richness, and a wisdom that can be found in meditation on the infinite void from which all phenomenal activity emerges.

Hacking the Universe

The self-help industry sprang from noble beginnings: providing inspiration and resources to help people take charge of their own lives. As the movement grew, many disciplines like *Neuro-Linguistic Programming*, the *Sedona Method*, *Be Set Free Fast*, and the *Emotional Freedom Technique*, as well as associated energy therapies, have been developed and have brought great benefits to many people.

But has the self-help movement now become more of a 'help yourself' industry? Many contemporary practitioners present the universe as an impersonal deity, which guards the door to a world of unlimited opportunity, wealth and enjoyment. People are encouraged to believe that the best and easiest way to enter this magical universe is through clever hacks, which will enable a person to dodge the patience, commitment and hard work required for any significant achievement.

This attitude is seen most prominently in the *Law of Attraction*. This concept has been discussed by celebrated New Thought authors like James Allen, Wallace D. Wattles, Napoleon Hill and Earl Nightingale. In its basic form, the observation that 'like attracts like' is quite reasonable. To become an expert golfer, one associates with golfers; to acquire the knowledge and skills required to practice medicine one learns from doctors; and to learn how to practice law, one studies with legal practitioners. Furthermore, in competitive arenas like sporting contests, one improves one's skills and builds a profile by vying with the 'best of the best' – the most intense form of association. On the other end of the scale, alcoholics congregate in bars, gambling addicts in casinos and drug addicts seek the company of dealers and fellow users.

In recent literature, most notably in the best-selling book and film *The Secret*, the recommended way to fulfil all one's desires is through the practice of intense imagination. *Don't plan; don't calculate; don't consider your opportunities or aptitudes; just imagine that you have achieved the coveted goal, rejoicing in the expected emotional reaction and vivid visualization of the experience of the achievement or possession – and the universe will find a way to deliver it to you.* Although there is a promise that one can satisfy any desire through this method, whether it be related to health, finance, travel, employment, possessions, acquisition of skills, or spiritual fulfilment, by far the heaviest emphasis is on the accumulation of wealth and enjoying the lifestyle of the rich and famous. In short: ask, expect and the Universe will deliver.

Understandably, the literature and seminar presentations provided by purveyors of this specious approach have been very popular with customers. It is an embarrassing human trait that we are attracted by the possibility of getting something for nothing, of great gains from minimal effort. We fantasize about winning the lottery, the sudden accession of undeserved wealth. Many of the techniques employed at these seminars are challenging and confrontational, and the resulting buzz that the attendee feels from successfully tackling something that is intimidating and strange persuades him of a great increase in personal power. The major obstacles blocking his achievement will simply be swept away, and that $5000 paid for the training has been money well spent. However, once the excitement dies down and the glow fades, the person discovers that he is essentially the same person, subject to the same fears and limitations.

This is not to say that the Law of Attraction is false; it is rather that its operation is much less crass than self-help mentors would encourage people to believe. A realistic and sadly humorous example is that of a man who desired great wealth and persistently affirmed to himself that he would find a job where he was regularly surrounded by great piles of money. His ambition was realized – he gained a position as a security guard in a bank vault. As James Allen has said, a person may know themself by their circumstances: look at the story of your life and you will see what you have attracted to yourself.

Deconstructing the Law of Attraction

The misinterpretation of the Law of Attraction is due to a misunderstanding of the reality behind the 'Should-Would-Could' principle. If the desired change in circumstances is based largely on activities in the 'would' category, reaching the goal is a reasonable expectation. If, on the other hand, realizing the ambition is dependent essentially on performing tasks that lie either in or beyond the 'could' category, the desired outcome is likely to remain a pipedream. To move from 'would' to 'could' in any area of activity, planning, patience and persistence are required. If you focus solely on visualizing your possession of a Ferrari, and take no practical steps to accumulate the funds required, the most likely outcome is that you will just become very proficient in imagining that you own a Ferrari.

Another flaw with the Law of Attraction is that its misapplication is not concordant with the second *Sign of Being* – Discontent. There is a presumption that a consistent state of enjoyable earthly satiety can be reached by the satisfaction of all desires. However, as we know, desires are endless. Even after the best meal, we will become hungry again. Furthermore, the enjoyment of great happiness can be lost through unpleasant circumstances. For instance, death will rob many people of the company of those they love dearly. We can also allow ourselves to be tormented by missing out on things that might have been – the fish that got away, or the business opportunity that landed in the lap of someone else.

The third, and perhaps most troubling issue with current applications of the Law of Attraction is the assumption that human beings can control their environment by thought alone. This is equivalent to suggesting that the shark controls the ocean through which he swims, or the eagle controls the air through which he flies. But these creatures become successful by *concordance* with the surrounding medium, not by trying to dominate it. In the same way, human beings are dependent on their environment and can only achieve what that environment permits. While the expanded range of choices available to us in comparison to the lower animals may create the illusion of vast personal power, we cannot decide to go without food, water, or air and survive for very long; nor can we, by choice, walk on water or fly through the air by flapping our arms. Therefore, our aim should be not to dominate the universe or to bring it to heel, but rather to learn how to navigate it joyfully and productively.

Appreciate and explore the opportunities that present themselves; eat the fruit which falls naturally from the tree. Remember that we are *gifted* with the use of things – we don't really own them. Our true nature cannot be gauged by our possessions. As W. C. Fields said, "A rich man is just a poor man with money."

Goal Setting

Setting goals may be seen as the process of turning activity into achievement, of organizing our activities to arrive at a predetermined conclusion.

The steps required to successfully achieve a goal can be laid as follows:

1. Definition – deciding what we want to do;
2. Planning – obtaining and organizing resources, including equipment, time and skills required;
3. Acting – performing the required tasks;
4. Assessment – evaluating the results of our efforts

In many cases, this process can be automatic. If a person is particularly committed to an activity and has a natural skill base, he or she may follow the process without apparent preliminary planning. In the case of an Olympic athlete, the steps may fall into a suitable pattern naturally: the athlete is so focused on his or her chosen sport that all the pieces just come together.

For those of us who are less gifted or more undecided when faced with a multitude of life choices, judicious setting of goals can be very useful.

It should always be borne in mind that the heart of the goal is the activity itself. If you want to paint your house, you would need first to choose a colour and acquire the paint and the appropriate equipment, but most of the time and effort will be spent actually applying the paint.

Defining a goal

A popular template for goal definition is the SMART acronym:

- **S**pecific
- **M**easurable
- **A**chievable
- **R**elevant
- **T**ime-based

In other words, the aspirant is encouraged to aim for a specific result that can be achieved within a fixed but realistic time frame. However, this model does not specify what an 'achievable goal' is.

An achievable goal might be understood as a goal whose achievement relies on the organization of existing resources, rather than requiring the acquisition of new resources.

Any goal setting should commence with a clearing of the mind – including removing the aim of attaining the 'remarkable.' For most of us, 'remarkable' usually equates to 'impossible'. The effortless performance of the violin virtuoso may appear astonishing to the non-musician, and the level of skill bewilderingly inaccessible. On the other hand, to the performer and to his professional colleagues, it is all in a day's work. To be achievable, a goal should represent something that could become a regular part of the person's daily life.

Referring to the "should-would-could" model, we can see that to achieve anything, we must build on our existing skills. In the normal course of events, children learn to crawl before they walk, and walk before they run. The stage of crawling progresses from a 'could' to a 'would', as do the succeeding stages of walking and running.

Hence the best set goals are those that are built on a selection of 'woulds', which lead to the new 'could', which can then become a new 'would'.

Goals vs Habits

Achieving a goal is different from acquiring a habit. A goal is a specific end; in contrast, a habit is a repeated pattern of behaviour. Acquiring a particular habit might be a goal – but achieving a particular goal is not a habit – although one can make a habit of achieving goals in general.

In the SMART template, the most important characteristic of any goal is that it is 'achievable'. This means that the goal is reasonable, and its achievement is congruent with the person's lifestyle. A classic example is the case of the person who wants to get fit. He buys a gym membership, attends a few sessions, finds himself intimidated by the exercise program, and feels very uncomfortable in the gym environment. Unsurprisingly, he loses motivation and his worthy goal becomes an addition to the waste bin of discarded efforts.

It would have been better for the person in this scenario to go to the gym *without* any expectations, exploring the options available to him before establishing a realistic goal based on a clear, concrete context and skill set. Once he felt enjoyment in the new routine and had become comfortable in the environment, he could set fitness goals with the confidence that he would achieve them. As a rule, people frequent gymnasiums because they like being there, not because they feel duty bound to improve themselves in an uncongenial environment.

Fascination

The acquisition of extreme skill starts with fascination. As a child, the great pianist Claudio Arrau refused to eat when he was denied access to a piano. Arrau's musical ability and dedication were such that he achieved much without setting obvious goals. Any attempt to make life meaningful and satisfying by arbitrarily setting personal goals is very unlikely to succeed. The real first step in goal setting, one which is rarely mentioned in motivation programs, is to learn to become fascinated. Once a driving passion for an activity is developed, a person will strive to keep doing it. Then, goal setting will become a natural outworking of passion, utilizing and organizing current skills in new ways to attain new outcomes.

Rewards can help in this process. The aspiring young piano student may love sitting at the keyboard and playing music, but may feel unenthusiastic about scales. The best way to address this is not for the student to force himself to practice such technical exercises for extended periods, but to start his practice with a short session of scales, with the promised reward of playing pieces afterward for as long as he likes. He may then begin to enjoy playing scales, and consequently develop a greater interest in them.

Once a goal has been achieved, it is in a sense, dead. If a tennis player aims to win a Wimbledon singles championship and achieves it, then the goal has served its purpose and is no longer operative. We should remember that we live long past the achievement or non-achievement of our goals. They do not define us – they are but stepping-stones on the path that winds into the mists of futurity.

Pathology

A good man knows his limitations

– Dirty Harry (Magnum Force)

Do you feel that your life is blighted by limitations? Are you eager to move forward? Are you keen to build a lifestyle that is satisfying and joyful?

In the Universal Declaration of Human Rights, issued by the United Nations in 1948, a number of "freedoms" were articulated, the primary aim being to define an ideal state of worldwide political and social equity, in which all would be free to pursue any acceptable personal goals. Such freedoms are designed to create a favourable environment for personal achievement. However, obstacles to success can be both external and internal: creation of a perfect arena for action does not ensure that such action will be successful. Just giving an inexperienced student of the violin a Stradivarius will not automatically turn him into a virtuoso.

It is tempting to believe that complete success in life can only be achieved by the satisfaction of all wants. Many self-help protocols are built on this assumption, the flaws of which become apparent on close examination.

To *want* is to desire something you don't have. An all-powerful being would have no *wants*, because it could instantly achieve whatever it desired. Human beings do not have absolute power. Discontent, as the *Second Sign of Being*, reminds us that we strive for achievement because we perceive the world and ourselves as imperfect and incomplete – everything is driven by an endless process of becoming.

Wanting is therefore inevitable. We accept that getting what we want will require, in many instances, considerable effort and inconvenience. But what if the path to achievement is blocked by impassable walls? How might we understand these absolute blocks?

An impassable wall – or not?

An 'impassable wall' offers an opportunity to examine the gap between aspiration and achievement. One of the first questions we might ask when encountering such a roadblock is:

Is this impassable wall existent by virtue of me (my nature) or the stars (circumstances)?

Here, the 'should-would-could' strategy can help. But first – note that there is one category of actions outside this model: 'the impossible'. We can daydream about things that, in a reasonable course of events, it is unlikely that we will ever do – climbing Mount Everest, flying to the Moon, winning a Nobel prize, or beating a world champion at chess or boxing. We can also fantasize about events that are possible, but which we think, in more sober moments, to be extremely unlikely –

winning the lottery or a miraculous recovery from a terminal illness. In such cases, this indulgent use of the faculty of imagination represents the 'next best thing' – we accept that we can't enjoy the experience in reality, and compensate by allowing ourselves to wallow in an ersatz feeling of accomplishment.

Hence, sometimes imagination can lead to action, and at other times, imagination can be a replacement for experience. The first step in analyzing psychological malaise is to establish how your imagination is being used. Assessing the gap between thought and action will help a person to identify their barriers to achievement.

A process

A good place to begin by asking three questions:

- What do I want?
- Is this a real need?
- What is stopping me from attaining this desire?

These questions can be seen as representing the following order:

- Definition
- Assessment
- Limitation

The next step is to review your habitual reactions as revealed in your history. By thorough and unsparing examination of your past actions, the boundaries set by your conception of acceptability of action will become clearer. For each person there are:

- Certain strong predilections
- Certain things that the person does not have the capacity to do
- Certain things that the person simply won't do

Here is the point at which the Three Action Choices model can be considered. An examination should allow a person to sort activities readily into the 'would' and 'could' categories. As those in the first category are easily repeatable, similar associated activities can be added to this category. Successful performance of an activity in the 'could' category is usually supported by the previous performance of a group of related activities in the 'would' category.

If your particular ambition involves multiple activities which you have never done before or that you find unpalatable, restructuring, or even redefining the goal should be considered. As a rule, the greater the proportion of 'woulds,' the more likely it is that the goal will be realized.

However, the issue remains that there are tasks that some people just don't like performing. If such aversion relates primarily to personal disinclination, rather than a genuine moral or legal objection or a physical impossibility, it can be worth examining the underlying activity pathology.

The treatment

In many cases activity pathology is addressable. The primary diagnosis should include consideration of the following questions:

- What do you like doing?
- What do you dislike doing?
- What would you absolutely not do?
- What disadvantages are you prepared to tolerate?
- Do you lack any of the necessary skills?

Then you can make the following assessment of the task in question:

- What would represent a successful completion?
- What are the benefits of a successful completion?
- What are the disadvantages of failure?

Summary

The basic rule of self-assessment can be summarized in the ancient Greek axiom:

Know Thyself

I would paraphrase this profoundly helpful recommendation as follows:

Know Thyself – warts and all

Activity is unavoidable. Life, even in repose, is constituted of constant movement. As the Bhavagad Gita (Chapter 3, Arnold translation) says:

No man shall 'scape from act

By shunning action; nay, and none shall come

By mere renouncements unto perfectness.

Nay, and no jot of time, at any time,

Rests any actionless; his nature's law

Compels him, even unwilling.

Therefore, it is vital that all your actions serve your best and most productive aspirations. If there is a hole in the sole of your shoe, patch it and keep walking.

Putting it all together

In its highest expression, religious practice in Hinduism, Taoism and Buddhism has a monistic focus: it is held that an essential oneness underlies all the fluctuations of the phenomenal world.

The most celebrated Taoist scripture, the Tao te Ching, opens with the following assertion. The translation used here is by Paul Carus, who chose to use the word "reason" for that usually rendered as "Tao."

The reason that can be reasoned is not the eternal Reason.
The name that can be named is not the eternal name.
The Unnameable is of heaven and earth the beginning.
The Nameable becomes of the ten thousand things the mother.

Therefore it is said:
"He who desireless is found
The spiritual of the world will sound.
But he who by desire is bound
Sees the mere shell of things around."

In a later verse, the Taoist sage says:

Reason begets unity; unity begets duality; duality begets trinity; and trinity begets the ten thousand things.

So, one may ask, can the components of Non-Expert Living be reconciled into a format where they support a unitary view of the human condition?

It so happens that by using the *Three Signs of Being* (Impermanence, discontent, non-self) as a basis, we can formulate a revealing view of human personality by aligning these with the other functional elements of Non-expert Living.

The Three Fires
- Attraction
- Aversion
- Ignorance

The Three Primary Desires
- Control
- Approval
- Security

The Three Action Choices
- Should
- Would
- Could

The following template shows the relationship between all these elements:

Sign of Being (Fire)	Source	Primary desire	Action choice
Impermanen	Attraction	Control	Could
Discontent	Aversion	Approval	Should
Non-self	Ignorance	Security	Would

While these principles are fixed in their nature, the result of their interplay is infinitely various.

Awareness of these principles should help you to evaluate your aspirations more effectively.

Impermanence

In the phenomenal world, we are all swept along in a river of ever-changing circumstances. We seek control of this turbulent situation by attracting or seeking appropriate objects and opportunities. As the associated activities are usually not immediately within reach, they fit into the 'could' category.

Discontent

Aversion can be defined as a negative response to particular objects or situations that evoke displeasure, disgust or opposition.

We feel that things that we don't like should either not exist or change – in other words, we don't approve of them. Hence, they relate to the 'should' category.

Non-self

Ignorance leads us to believe that we have an enduring core of personality, and an identity in which we feel secure. We bolster this sense by the performance of habitual and easy actions. These fall naturally into the 'would' category.

Practical Application

As the *Bhavagad Gita* states, no person can abstain from action. Even a comatose patient in a hospital displays a degree of activity, although all of it is involuntary. In a waking state, conscious action is unavoidable.

 The action template shown above in this chapter is designed to help people to clarify:

- Their motivation
- Their expectations
- Their capacities

For the appropriate choice of action, a person needs to answer the following questions:

- Why do I want to perform this action?
- What are the expected results of the action?
- What are the benefits and disadvantages of the action?
- Do I have what it takes to perform the task successfully?

The prime tool in effective performance is self-knowledge:

- Knowing how to do something
- Know why you are doing the task
- Knowing how well you are likely to do the task

For life to be joyful and productive, the selection and performance of activities need to be optimized. Choose wisely – act effectively. It is my hope that applying the principles of Non-Expert Living will help you to do so.

The Art of Non-Expert Living – Oberon Michaels

Chapter 5: Meditation

Meditation and visualization

What is meditation? Consider the following:

- Meditation is not a state of mind, but rather an activity that produces a state of mind;
- Meditation enables the practitioner to develop a deeper and more comprehensive understanding of their true self.

Meditation is a method of dynamic introspection. Its eventual aim is the total integration of the subject (you, the seer), the object (that which is seen), and the process of seeing. Subject, object and process become, through meditation, a unified experience.

While there is a vital link between concentration and meditation, they are not the same. Concentration involves narrowing one's focus onto a particular activity or entity and sustaining that focus. Meditation requires concentration, but one can concentrate without meditating. An object of concentration may be internal or external, but in most cases, the object retains its identity as a discrete entity. In contrast, meditation aims at a state of complete but conscious absorption in which no awareness of separateness remains, and all elements coalesce into an indissoluble wholeness.

Fundamental principles of meditation

While meditation techniques are many and varied, the fundamental principles remain constant. Confusion arises when intellectual or psycho-physical activities are mistakenly described as meditation. To meditate effectively, the following requirements must be satisfied:

- Correct posture: a seated position, which can be maintained without undue stress or discomfort, and in which the back is kept straight, head upright, and neck, shoulders and abdomen remain relaxed. A prone posture is unsuitable as it is too conducive to sleep. A standing posture has insufficient balance and involves too much active concentration for easy maintenance of stability.

- Correct respiration: the flow of the breath should be regular, steady and not overstimulated, restricted, or suppressed in any way. In most cases it should be allowed to proceed in its own rhythm, the meditator observing but not interfering in the process.

- Correct focus: eyes are usually closed, with the eyelids relaxed. It is essential that outside distractions are minimized. As seventy percent of sensory input to the brain is through vision, closing your eyes is the most effective immediate step in reducing obvious distractions.

- Correct attention: meditation is characterized by an attitude of assertive passivity in which one observes phenomena with total intensity without seeking in any way to alter or interfere with the entity under scrutiny.

· Correct environment: a clean, quiet and comfortable space, where the meditator can be alone and is not subject to interruptions.

· Correct attire: clothing should be light, loose and comfortable. One should not be aware of the texture of the fabrics or the weight of the clothes.

Understanding meditation

To fully understand the process of meditation, we need to examine the cultures from which it sprang. Meditation is the central practice in Hinduism and Buddhism, the major religions of the far East. In this religious milieu, meditation is not used as a way to 'get high', but rather to strip away the veils that obscure a person's vision of reality. When one attains a true perception of reality, one will understand that the phenomenal world is unstable, in a state of perpetual change, and subject to an infinite variety of influences. Faced with this process of constant and ineluctable change, one seeks a sense of genuine stability and security. Independence of mind and action, or, in other words, release from the infinite circumstantial chain of events, can only be attained when one is able to see the phenomenal world as it really is: *a world of shadows, existing only in the mind of the beholder.*

Meditation is the most practical and efficient tool for seeking this state of elevated awareness. All that is needed is the mind and will of the practitioner: props, ceremonies, dogma, and intercessions or directions made by a third party are not only unnecessary but in fact create impediments in the meditation process. Meditation is the ultimate self-help strategy, and for this reason, is often viewed with distrust by Western religious organizations with their vast tables of dogma and hierarchies of clergy. No one willingly subscribes to an activity or organization that he doesn't need, and meditation is a profoundly effective method of defining and minimizing one's needs.

Two views of meditation

'Diving' is one image that can help us understand meditation. If one dives deep into the inner self, one finds at first an almost impenetrable darkness, physical and psychological. Masters of meditation assure us, however, that with persistent repetition of valid meditation exercises, one eventually finds the "pearl of great price" – a pervasive state of joy and clarity, in which division and conflict resolve themselves quickly and naturally. A more contemporary definition of this state might describe it as a balanced and positive state, free from any trauma, violent impulse or inhibition, and imbued with a sense of power and peace. The darkness that appears to surround the novice when he first closes his eyes in meditation is in fact a cloak created by his mind with its fears and prejudices; the light exists, but he must remove the obstacle to his inner vision. He is the only person that can remove that obstacle, and he must want to do it.

The other useful image is that of a mountain. As one climbs the mountain, one's view expands, and, on reaching the top, one has a full view not only of the land below but also of the path that one has taken. In the early stages, the path that gives access to the peak may be difficult to find, and may involve a lengthy and frustrating search which leads to many dead ends. However, the closer one gets to the peak, the clearer the path becomes. It may become also more arduous, steep, and full of obstacles that cannot be evaded without going backwards. On the other hand, the more established one is in the path, the less likely one is to abandon it.

Eastern and Western approaches

The mountain image is also useful in understanding the differences between Eastern and Western approaches to inner experience. The Easterner will accept the mountain for what it is: an obstacle that has to be climbed. He also accepts the view that each person must do his own climbing: no one can arrive at the top vicariously. On the other hand, the Westerner, seduced by his own ingenuity, may seek either to make the mountain easier to climb by installing an escalator, or might want to remove the mountain altogether. He may argue that everyone is entitled to the splendid view from the top, and the person who can help others enjoy the view with a minimum of effort and expenditure of time is doing society a great service.

A comparison of these views is useful in demonstrating the power of meditation. Possession of an encyclopedia does not confer knowledge just as flying over a mountain in a helicopter will not teach people the skills of mountain climbing. Facts in isolation are dead and meaningless; command of any discipline requires not only sufficient factual knowledge but *also* the understanding to assemble that knowledge and derive practical experience from it. The average educated Westerner sitting in a meditation session is ludicrously over-qualified for the activity on an intellectual level; all that is needed is a body in good health, knowledge of the meditation technique, and the will to practise it. All the material and intellectual associations the Westerner carries with him are in fact an impediment. To return to the scaling of our hypothetical mountain, the Easterner merely requires the body and the will to climb. To build his escalator the Westerner requires a vast labour force, engineering and materials technology, finance, and (often) political support all to be available before the first client begins his ascent.

Satisfaction

The more immediately physical an activity is, the more satisfying and empowering it can be. Climbing a mountain on foot may be an arduous and time-consuming process, but it will the memory will vividly remain with the climber and add richness to her view of life. The more labour-saving technology that is interposed between the person and the pursuit of her goal, the less informative, memorable and satisfying the experience will be. The ultimate extension of our mountain climbing scenario is the person watching others move up the escalator *on television*. The television camera may give splendid coverage of the view from the top, but to our viewer comfortably ensconced in his loungeroom, this picture will probably be no more exciting or informative than that of a jar of coffee beans in the next commercial.

Direct involvement is the key to knowledge and skill acquisition. Meditation is the inner journey in which one strives for that inner awareness that can connect one immediately to anything the mind cognizes. It is said that in the highest meditative state, one has immediate access to all one's memories and knowledge. The tedious process of constantly reconstructing the world to suit one's fears and prejudices is no longer necessary, and the master practitioner becomes truly liberated.

Visualization

Visualization can be employed for two basic purposes:

- To relax and recharge the body
- To aid in the acquisition of a particular skill or outcome

Visualization to develop a particular aptitude or advance in skill is employed by sports people and performers and in this application is best undertaken under the guidance of a trained therapist.

While cultivating a meditative attitude of peace is necessary for effective visualization, it should not be considered to be true meditation. While the two practices share the cultivation of the awareness of being an observer, visualization is essentially an enabling practice rather than a purely ontological exploration.

Many of the practices of introspection recommended by Christian churches are in fact forms of visualization. The devotee is encouraged to 'meditate' on an incident in the Gospels or on the virtues of a particular saint, the object being to develop an intense sense of piety. Therefore, the attention is to be directed towards an external image or artefact, rather than plunging deeply into the inner self.

Now you try

A simple meditation technique:

Sit in a comfortable position. A seated yoga pose, such as the lotus position, can be used if you are capable of sustaining it without excessive effort. Seiza (simple diamond pose in yoga terminology) is also suitable, although the legs tend to go to sleep fairly quickly in this position. Otherwise, one may sit in a chair, making sure that the seat is low enough so that the soles of the feet rest on the floor.

Keep your back straight, head held level, and neck, shoulders and abdomen relaxed.

Is your environment pleasant and uncluttered? Is the ambient temperature comfortable, but not warm? (Warmth can encourage sleepiness). Surroundings should be quiet, and arranged to exclude music or distracting noises.

Softly close your eyes. Release all tension in your face. Keep your mouth closed, with your upper and lower teeth slightly apart and your tongue resting loosely at the bottom of your mouth.

When you are settled in your posture, begin to observe your breath. Allow it to flow in and out without any effort to regulate or restrict it.

As thoughts float into your mind, observe them with detachment. Make no effort either to suppress them or to follow them. As each thought floats away, gently return your attention to your breath.

Regular bursts of short meditation practice will be much more effective than sporadic sessions of greater length. Ten minutes twice a day every day will bring substantial benefits. The simplicity of meditation techniques is part of their effectiveness. Anyone can practise this technique. The quality and frequency of the practice are entirely up to the practitioner.

Where to learn to meditate.

Many organizations, religious and cultural, provide meditation training. When looking for instruction in meditation, consider:

- What form of meditation you wish to practise;
- What sort of organization or environment is most suitable for your needs.

Some organizations have a requirement that the student pledge not to reveal their meditation techniques to others. The reason for this practice is generally to protect the techniques from corruption or misuse by unauthorized practitioners; it does not always indicate a desire to brainwash or mislead the intending student. However, students should be wary of any organizations that make the following demands:

- Unreasonable dedication or submissiveness;
- Extravagant or harsh changes in the student's lifestyle;
- Large sums of money as gifts', tuition fees, or membership subscriptions;
- Slavish adherence to any creed or dogma (discouragement of questions or individual thinking);
- Affiliation with outside political and cultural organizations;
- Forcible recruiting of friends or associates to the organization.

Meditation is a personal and private practice. Practitioners should be free either to disclose or not to disclose their meditation activities as they wish.

The Art of Non-Expert Living – Oberon Michaels

Conclusion

Goodbye for now

Thank you for considering my ideas, as presented in *Non-Expert Living*. You are free to disagree with any of the interpretations of religion I have offered or the conclusions that I have drawn. The opinions expressed and the strategies suggested have worked well for me, and, to my mind, have been respectful and supportive of others. However, I acknowledge that every life is an individual path, and that approaches that have not suited me may work very well for others (and vice versa)

There is one piece of wisdom that anyone can apply to good effect:

If something looks too good to be true, it probably is.

Most problems have solutions, but seeking a solution that will resolve all personal problems forever is futile and frustrating. Apart from death, there is nothing that can remove all sources of discontent from your life. The best way to live is to embrace the apparent imperfections in the world in the knowledge that all things, good and bad, will pass.

I do not claim expertise in any area. I respect and encourage the appropriate employment of recognized experts as an aspect of a well-regulated life. However, the role of the expert is to offer well-informed advice, and where applicable, to act on the decisions of the recipient. Experts advise, but you decide – and bear the consequences.

The search for pleasure and purpose is a fundamental aspect of the human condition. People will always want things; the key to a good life is not to *stop* wanting, which is impossible, but to cease being dominated by one's wants. Learn to be happy in your discontent and restrained in your moments of glory.

Desires can be educated. It can be argued that most actions, even the most heinous, are intended to produce some sort of beneficial outcome, even if it be for only one person. We have a natural impulse to believe that if we were able to reconstruct the world around us, it would become a better place. The most noble goal is to change the world in a way that benefits the greatest number of people and causes disadvantage to the least. We can learn to focus on those attitudes and activities which nourish the most uplifting aspirations in everyone that we encounter.

Religious apologists are fond of urging their subscribers to "fight the darkness." However, darkness is only an absence of light: once light is introduced it vanishes. As Jesus says in the Gospel of Matthew (Chapter 5, verses 14-16)

Ye are the light of the world. A city that is set on an hill cannot be hid.

Neither do men light a candle, and put it under a bushel, but on a candlestick; and it giveth light unto all that are in the house.

Let your light so shine before men, that they may see your good works, and glorify your Father which is in heaven.

The following saying has been attributed in error to Mahatma Gandhi, but regardless of its source, it remains a powerfully productive piece of advice:

Be the change you wish to see in the world.

I would like to conclude with the words of New Thought author, James Allen, from the preface of his classic treatise on the power of thought, *As A Man Thinketh*:

Mind is the Master power that moulds and makes,
And Man is Mind, and evermore he takes
The tool of Thought, and, shaping what he wills,
Brings forth a thousand joys, a thousand ills:
He thinks in secret, and it comes to pass:
Environment is but his looking-glass.

Bibliography

All biblical quotations have been taken from the King James Version (1611, public domain).

Several citations have been made from the Catholic Encyclopedia, The Encyclopedia Press, New York, 1913.

Aiken, C. F. "Buddhism", *Catholic Encyclopedia*. New York: Robert Appleton, 1908.

Alighieri, Dante. *The Divine Comedy of Dante Alighieri. Translated by Charles Eliot Norton*. Boston: Houghton Mifflin, 1902.

Allen, James. *As a Man Thinketh*, New York: Thomas Y. Crowell company, 1913.

Arnold, Sir Edwin. *The Song Celestial or Bhagavad-Gita (From the Mahabharata)*, New York: Truslove, Hanson & Comba, Ltd, 1900.

Byrne, Rhonda. *The Secret.* Cammeray NSW: Simon & Schuster Australia, 2006.

Carus, Paul. *The Canon of Reason and Virtue (Lao-Tze's Tao the King)*. Chicago: The Open Court Pub. Company, 1903.

Carus, Paul. *The Gospel of Buddha*. Chicago & London: The Open Court Publishing Company, 1894.

Carus, Paul. *The History of the Devil and the Idea of Evil.* Chicago: The Open Court Publishing Company, 1900.

Chang, Garma C.C. *The Practice of Zen*. San Francisco: Harper and Row, 1970.

Dawkins, Richard. *The God Delusion.* New York: Mariner Books, Harper Collins, 2006.

Dawood, N. J. *The Koran.* London: Penguin Books, 2003.

Del Castillo, Bernal Diaz, Lockhart, John Ingram. *The Memoirs of the Conquistador Bernal Diaz Del Castillo.* London: J. Hatchard and Son, 1844

Dryden, John. *Virgil's Æneid.* London: George Routledge and Sons, 1884.

Dwoskin, Hale. *The Sedona Method.* Minnetonka, Minnesota: Sedona Press, 2003.

Eker, T. Harv. *Secrets of the Millionaire Mind.* New York: Harper Business, 2005.

Eliot, Thomas Stearns. *Four Quartets.* London: Faber and Faber, 1944.

Gibbons, James. *The Faith of Our Fathers.* Baltimore: John Murphy company, 1905.

Herigel, E. *Zen in the Art of Archery.* Oxfordshire, UK: Routledge, 1972.

Humphreys, Christmas. *Buddhism – An Introduction and Guide.* London: Penguin Books, 1951.

Humphreys, Christmas. *Zen Buddhism.* London: Allen & Unwin, 1962.

Khayyám, Omar. *The Rubáiyát of Omar Khayyám,* Translated by Edward FitzGerald. Bernard Quaritch: London,1879.

Krauss, Laurence M. *A Universe From Nothing.* New York: Simon & Schuster, 2012.

Leggett, Trevor. *A First Zen Reader.* Tokyo: Tuttle, 1960.

Levenson, Lester. *No Attachments, No Aversions*. Sherman Oakes, CA: Lawrence Crane Enterprises, 2003.

Levenson, Lester and Dwoskin, Hale. *Happiness Is Free,* Minnetonka, Minnesota: Sedona Press, 2020.

Max Müller, F. *The Dhammapada, From Sacred Books of the East, Volume 10*, Oxford: Oxford University Press, 1881.

Pius IX, Pope, *Quanta Cura and The Syllabus of Errors,* Kansas City, Missouri: Angelus Press, 1998.

Rodwell, J. M. (John Medows), *The Koran,* London & Toronto: E P Dutton & Co, 1909.

O'Brien, John A. *The Faith of Millions*. Huntington, Ind.: Our Sunday Visitor, 1955.

Ratzinger, Joseph. "Homily" 18 April 2005. Rome: Vatican Basilica.

Shaku, Soyen, *Sermons of a Buddhist Abbot*. Chicago: The Open Court Publishing Company, 1906.

Smith, Lloyd E. *Dialogues of Plato*. Kansas: Haldeman-Julius, 1924.

Suzuki, D. T. *Essays in Zen Buddhism*, Volumes 1–3. London: Rider, 1970.

———. *Introduction to Zen Buddhism*. London: Rider, 1969.

———. *Manual of Zen Buddhism*. London: Rider, 1950.

———.*The Zen Doctrine of No Mind*. London: Rider, 1969.

Suzuki, Shunryu. *Zen Mind, Beginner's Mind*. New York: Weatherhill, 1972.

Tichenor, Henry M. *The Buddhist Philosophy of Life*. Kansas: Haldeman-Julius, 1924.

Von Cochem, Martin. *The Four Last Things: Death, Judgment, Hell, Heaven.* New York: Benziger, 1899.

Watts, Alan. *The Way of Zen*. London: Penguin, 1970.

Wright, Dudley. *A Manual of Buddhism*. London: Kegan, Paul, Trench, Trübner and Co., 1912.

www.ingramcontent.com/pod-product-compliance
Lightning Source LLC
Chambersburg PA
CBHW041324110526
44592CB00021B/2808